THE AI REAL ESTATE MILLIONAIRE

The Complete Guide to Investing in Net Leased Commercial Properties with No Landlord Expense or Responsibility

by

Hank Levine

HOLLYHILL PUBLISHING

The Armchair Real Estate Millionaire
The Complete Guide to Investing In Net Leased Commercial Properties With No Landlord Expense or Responsibility
by Hank Levine

Copyright © 2005 by
Hollyhill Publishing
P.O. Box 532
Hendersonville, TN 37077.

This publication is designed to provide accurate and authoritative information in regard to the subject matter covered. It is sold with the understanding that the publisher is not engaged in rendering legal, accounting or other professional service. If legal advice or other expert assistance is required, the services of a competent professional person should be sought.
—*from a Declaration of Principle jointly adopted by a committee of the American Bar Association and a committee of publishers.*

Library of Congress Cataloging-In-Publication Data
Levine, Hank
The Armchair Real Estate Millionaire : the complete guide to investing in net leased commercial properties with no landlord expense or responsibility / by Hank Levine
p. cm.
Includes Index
LCCN 2005923076
ISBN 0-9767034-0-8

1. Real estate investment. I. Title
HD1382.5.L485 2005   332.63'24
QB105-200090

Cover and book design by Norm Kale, PR Omni Digital, Nashville, TN
Edited by Ira Penn, Bellingham, WA

DISCLAIMER

The topics covered in this book are designed to provide helpful information about Net Lease Investing. It is sold with the understanding that the author is solely a Real Estate Broker and does not engage in rendering legal, accounting or other professional services. If legal, accounting or other expert assistance is required the services of a competent professional should be sought. Care has been taken to provide a clear and accurate presentation of the subject matter in this book, however the author and publisher do not assume any legal liability or responsibility for any loss or damage alleged to be caused by the information presented.

If you do not wish to be bound by the above, you may return this book to the publisher for a full refund.

Dedicated to Mariana
My wife, my lifelong companion, and my best friend.
This book could not have been possible wihout her
continuing encouragement and support.

Also thanks to: *Norm Kale, PR Omni Digital,* who not only designed and printed the book but was my patient mentor, guiding me through the labyrinth of self-publishing from the first baby steps to the final product; *Ira Penn, Bellingham, Washington,* my dear friend and editor, who made sure that I not only dotted the I's and crossed the T's, but also placed the periods securely within the quotation marks.

INTRODUCTION
Too Good to be True?

Many of the investors who contact me regarding the prospective purchase of a Commercial Real Estate property currently own one or a number of residential rental houses. They are deeply involved in "Property Management." They pay the taxes and insurance on their properties, collect rents, and are responsible for all maintenance, including plumbing, electrical, landscaping, roofing, general repairs, etc.

They may often do the work themselves if they have the necessary skills. This means that when they bought the property for investment purposes they also bought themselves a job. Some of them have hired a property management company to do all this for them in return for 10% of the gross rent. That's 10% of their anticipated profit going to someone else. Often the management company is earning more on their investment than they are!

Then I explain to them the advantages of owning a Net Leased Commercial Property: Absolutely no management responsibilities with their Tenant paying all taxes, insurance and doing all the maintenance. The investor's only two duties each month are to deposit the rent check and pay the mortgage note. The difference between the two is their monthly cash return. In addition, with their Tenant's rent, which increases over time, plus their equity buildup, which increases monthly, they can anticipate a return of fifteen to twenty percent on their cash down payment starting year one and increasing annually. Invariably their response is, "But that sounds too good to be true!"

In this book I will show you that it is absolutely true and is the safe, sure and easy way to separate "work" from "investment" and to become an "Armchair Real Estate Millionaire"

Contents

PART II – Beyond the Basics

PART I

THE BASICS

A QUICK GUIDE TO TRIPLE NET INVESTMENTS

*In my Net Lease Workshop*s for new investors or those unfamiliar with "Net Lease" I usually begin with an overview of the subject — a brief definition of Triple Nets, what they are, why they are available, what kind of return to expect and, in general, how Net Lease works and differs from other real estate investments. Although not especially complex, there are many areas to cover in detail. This overview will give you a foundation on which to build a complete understanding of Net Lease investing and to decide if it is right for you.

THE OVERVIEW

Many large corporations prefer to lease rather than own their buildings for two reasons: they can only depreciate the cost of the building over 39 years, and it remains as a long-term debt on their books. The monthly rent payment is written off as an annual expense on their tax return. Therefore they often have a building custom built and sell it with a long-term lease in place. The return to the investor/purchaser is excellent —- usually starting at around 15% to 20% and going up annually over the term of the lease because of periodic rent raises and the equity build-up.

The Leases are called "Triple Net", which means the Tenant is responsible for all repairs and maintenance — including capital items (roof, structure, parking lot, landscaping, etc.). In addition, he pays all property taxes and insurance. The Landlord has no expense or responsibility.

Most investors will purchase a Net Leased property by leveraging their cash outlay —- putting twenty to twenty-five percent down and obtaining a long-term bank loan for the balance. The Tenant's rent payment covers the mortgage note and in addition provides a steady, excellent monthly cash return.

Leases are usually from ten to twenty years with additional option periods. The NNN property is invariably a single-tenant, free-standing building. And since it is occupied by an "investment grade" company such as General Electric, Walgreen Drug, KFC, Circuit City, etc. there is little likelihood of default.

Because of the financial standing of the Tenant, long-term bank loans are usually obtained at a more favorable interest rate and lower down payment than with other kinds of commercial real estate investments. This allows the investor to acquire the property with fewer dollars up front. In addition, the property's potential rise in value over time because of its prime commercial location is a big plus.

Although most investors prefer properties that are not more than two to three hours driving time from their homes, they will have a much larger selection of currently available properties if they can include other cities in which they have business or family connections, occasionally visit, or to which perhaps they would eventually like to retire.

Now, the details.........

LEASES
They Define Your Return

There are two factors which will determine the profitability of your investment in Net Leased property – the terms of your bank loan and the Lease. This document sets out all the conditions of your Tenant's occupancy; the number of years in the initial (primary) term, the option periods, the annual rent payment and the time and amount of rent increases or percentage rent. It defines the Tenant's obligation for taxes, insurance and maintenance and specifies the guarantor of the Lease payment (the rent). From it you will calculate the overall return on your investment.

The Lease often runs to fifteen or twenty pages or more and you will need to be familiar with all its details before you agree to purchase the property. Both Landlord and Tenant are legally bound by all the terms of the Lease for its duration and it remains in effect even if the property is sold. The Tenant must still continue to pay the agreed upon rent even if for some reason the property becomes vacant. Responsibility for the three major expenses involved in property ownership — taxes, insurance and maintenance, are defined by the Lease.

We will next examine the various Lease types as well as some of the terms included in them, such as Options, Rent Increases, Termination Rights and Percentage Rent.

The **Gross Lease** is the most basic type of Lease and is the one most familiar to residential renters who pay a fixed amount monthly to the Landlord. The Lease may be for a defined length of time, or, if no specific time is noted, will be from month-to-month. In a month-to-month Lease occupancy continues until a thirty day notice is given by either party. The Lease may contain various conditions of occupancy (no pets, noise restrictions, etc.) but the property's Landlord pays all major expenses. The Tenant's sole financial responsibility is a timely payment of the rent.

Net Lease is a general term for those Leases which obligate the Tenant to pay one or all of the three major expenses. The Lease most beneficial to the property owner is the **Triple Net Lease (NNN)** in which the Tenant pays taxes, insurance, and is responsible for all maintenance of any nature. This may include repairs to the roof, foundation, heating/air conditioning systems (HVAC), landscaping, parking area or anything else needed to keep the property in good condition. There are no Landlord expenses or obligations whatsoever.

Even more desirable is the **Absolute Bond Triple Net Lease** which adds the Tenant's obligation for casualty (fire and wind damage), condemnation and even Eminent Domain. It is often referred to as the "hell or high water" Lease, because the Tenant agrees to pay rent no matter what, with no rental stream interruption for any reason whatsoever.

There are Leases in which the Tenant pays taxes and insurance but the Landlord is responsible for some elements of the property's upkeep. Although these obligations vary from Lease to Lease, the most common are the responsibility for the building's structural integrity such as the roof, foundation and outside walls (not including glass). This is known as a **Double Net** or **Net Net Lease (NN).**

Another type is the **Ground Lease** in which the investor owns the land but not the building that is on it (the improvement). He receives a rent check monthly or annually from the owner/operator of that business for the duration of the Lease Term, which could be 25 or 50 or 99 years. There are obviously no Landlord responsibilities or expenses and property taxes are paid by the Tenant. At the termination of the Ground Lease the rights to any improvements revert to the land owner. Because of the absolute safety of this type of investment the percentage return is often one to two points lower than for a Triple Net Lease.

The **Commencement Date** of the Lease is the initial

date when the Tenant's rent started. An investor may purchase a property in the ninth year of a twenty year Primary Lease, meaning that it has eleven more years to run before its expiration. However, the Lease may contain provisions for the Tenant to continue in business for a number of years at that location after the Primary Lease has expired. These rights are known as **Options.** They are quite often in five year increments, and any rise in the rent payments during these option periods are negotiated in advance and are part of the Lease Agreement.

Often Commercial Leases will include provisions for **Percentage Rent,** the Tenant's payment to the Landlord of a fixed percentage of the annual sales at that location, in addition to the monthly rent. Percentage Rent may start in the first year of the Lease or may occur later in the Lease period when the Tenant has achieved a sales volume over a specified, pre-determined gross amount known as the **Break Point.** It is normally paid annually in one lump sum, usually about two to three months after either the beginning of the next calendar year or the Tenant's fiscal year when all the sales results for the previous year are tallied. The Landlord has the right to audit his Tenant's books if he feels that the amount reported may be incorrect.

Occasionally a **Termination Right** is seen in Net Leases. This is when the Tenant has a firm ten year Lease but would like to retain the option to vacate the property and terminate the Lease at the end of its fifth year. In this instance, the Tenant is normally required to give from two to six months advance notice that he will be exercising this option and must pay a penalty equal to 24 to 30 months rent. This penalty is due and payable with the notice and, once given, is not refundable even if the Tenant changes his mind during the notice period and would now like to stay for the full Lease term.

For the Landlord who has a very desirable commercial location and is able to find a new Tenant at the same or perhaps even better terms in a relatively short time this could be a very desirable situation, for he will receive the penalty and, in addition, will also receive rent from his new Tenant. The worst case scenario is that he will have the notice period plus at least two years to find a new Tenant while he retains an amount equal the former occupant's rent. The Termination Right is also known as **a Kick-Out Clause.**

Many Leases also include periodic rent increases usually referred to as **Rent Bumps.** They are often in five-year increments, but could occur annually or bi-annually. A common rent increase might be five, eight or ten percent every five years, or perhaps one or two percent annually. It is sometime tied to the annual rise in the government's Consumer Price Index (CPI). This is the ultimate in inflation protection for the investor and another reason why Net Leased Commercial Properties, in addition to being Armchair Investments, are the safest investments available.

A Quick Review of Chapter 2

The investor's bank loan and the terms of the Lease determine the profitability of his investment in Net Leased properties.

The Lease defines the length and conditions of the Tenant's occupancy, his rent payments and his responsibility for taxes, insurance and maintenance.

TERMS

Gross Lease – Tenant pays a fixed monthly amount to Landlord. Has no obligation for expenses.

Net Lease – Tenant pays one or all of the property's expenses.

Double Net (NN) - Tenant pays taxes and insurance. Landlord pays for some elements of the property's upkeep.

Triple Net (NNN) – Tenant pays taxes, insurance and is responsible for all maintenance.

Absolute Triple Net Lease – Adds Tenant's responsibility for casualty (fire & wind damage).

Ground Lease – Investor owns the land but does not own the building until Lease expires.

Commencement Date – Initial date of Tenant's rent payment.

Percentage Rent – Tenant's obligation to pay Landlord a fixed percentage of gross annual sales in addition to monthly rent.

Termination Right – Tenant's option to terminate Lease before end of the primary Lease term in return for a monetary penalty.

Rent Bumps – Periodic rent increases during the term of a Commercial Lease.

3

FINANCING 101

The financing of your Net Lease purchase is perhaps the most critical factor in obtaining the maximum return on your investment. In this chapter we introduce a number of terms you need to know, along with other aspects of financing that will help you to fully understand this important subject. If you own rental properties you may already be familiar with some of these terms:

- Cap Rate
- Market Rent
- Return on Investment (ROI)
- Cash on Cash
- Net Operating Income (NOI)
- Equity Buildup
- Assumable Loan
- Five Year Call
- Balloon
- Adjustable Rate Mortgage (ARM)

Perhaps the most important term for the Net Lease investor is the **CAP Rate** (short for "Capitalization

Rate"). This is simply the percentage return on his initial cash outlay or cash down payment. For example, if you were to receive ten thousand dollars annually on a $100,000 investment it would be a ten percent return, or a "Ten CAP" ($10,000 divided by $100,000 = 10%). If you received only nine thousand dollars it would be a nine percent return, or a "Nine CAP", etc. *In a Net Lease investment the CAP Rate is the annual rent divided by the purchase price.*

CAP Rates on some Net Leased properties are as low as six percent (or even lower) while on other properties they may be eight to ten percent (or higher). The reason is "Supply and Demand." At any one time there are more investors looking for Triple Nets than there are properties available, especially those priced at less than one million dollars.

Another factor is that commercial Tenants, being in business to make the most money possible, would like to pay as little rent as possible. Therefore many of the most desirable properties sometimes offer the smallest annual dollar returns since the Tenants are often paying less than **"Market Rent"** — *the average cost per square foot for a similar type of business in a comparable location.* These "in demand" companies are well aware that they can attract buyers with the least possible impact on their bottom line.

For example, a Walgreen Drug in a prime location with a twenty or twenty-five year Absolute Bond Triple

Net Lease and three ten–year options is probably one of the best and safest long-range portfolio investments available, even with no rent bumps until the option periods. Walgreen's CAP Rate often is in a six to six and one half percent range. In addition, there are usually very few of them available at any one time. Even at three to four million dollars (and sometimes higher) they are often sold in a matter of weeks!

Another large factor impacting CAP Rates is the number of years remaining on the Tenant's primary Lease term. It is much more difficult to sell a property, no matter how desirable, with only three or four years until its expiration. A potential buyer cannot be certain that the Tenant, at the expiration of his Lease period, will want to stay in business at that location and be willing to renew the Lease or pick up the Option Periods. He will naturally wonder if he will be stuck with an empty building.

So in order to move this property the seller, most often a private party who has owned the building since the Lease's inception, will need to increase the return to a Nine or Ten CAP (or even higher) with the hope that a potential buyer will assume that the present Tenant will renew the Lease before its termination or pick up the Option Period. Lacking that, the buyer must feel that the location is so excellent he will be able to obtain another long-term Tenant for that property in a reasonable period of time.

The CAP Rate, along with the financing of the investment is a vital factor in calculating the **Return on Investment (ROI)** —- *the percentage or monetary return on the cash down-payment.* But it is also important to note that with periodic rent bumps over the length of the Lease the CAP Rate will keep on increasing, since the original purchase price remains the same while the rent payment goes up. *The new CAP Rate will equal the current increased rent divided by the purchase price.*

An initial "Seven CAP" over time may therefore become a "Nine" or "Ten CAP" by the end of the Lease period. With this in mind, some long-term investors are willing to accept a lower CAP Rate on an excellent Credit Tenant property in a terrific location with steady rent bumps. They know that by Lease year five or six the increasing return (plus the anticipated appreciation on the property) will more than make up for the lower cash flow in the first years of the Lease.

Cash-On-Cash is the dollar return on the investor's cash down-payment —- the annual amount he has kept after depositing his rent checks and making the payments on his mortgage *expressed in dollars instead of percent.* For example, ten thousand dollars back on a $100,000 investment is $10,000 Cash-On-Cash.

Net Operating Income (NOI) is *the annual cash return after deducting operating expenses (taxes, insurance and maintenance) from the annual rent.* In a Triple Net property there are no operating expenses, since they are all paid by the Tenant, so the NOI is simply the annual rent payment. Income taxes and depreciation are not included in calculating the NOI since they are not "operating expenses." On a Double Net property where there are some Landlord expenses, these obligations are first deducted from the rent payment to obtain the Net Operating Income.

The **Equity Buildup** is a large part of the Return on Investment (ROI). It normally will add ten percent or more to the investor's total return in the first year, and both the Equity Buildup and the total return keep growing annually. *It is the steadily increasing principal part of the "interest and principal" in a monthly bank payment.* In a Net Leased investment, in addition to providing an income, the Tenant is also buying the property for the investor with his rent payments since the monthly rent check pays both the principal and interest on his note.

Some available Triple Net properties will already have in place loans which were obtained by the present owners when they first purchased the property. They are often **assumable** by a potential buyer with good credit. Would this be a good deal for the buyer? Yes and No. If the interest rate is in line with or lower than current rates, the seller is willing to absorb a possible pay-off penalty, and there is not an excessive cash down-payment, it would be an excellent opportunity to purchase the property without going through the process of negotiating a new loan and paying origination fees, points and other bank charges.

However, if it is possible to obtain a new loan one to

two percentage points (or more) lower than the loan in place, the investor would obviously be better off not assuming the current one. If it must be assumed as a condition of sale it is usually better to pass on the property unless the terms are quite favorable. Because of that these properties will often offer a higher CAP Rate. But most investors prefer to purchase a Net Leased property by obtaining their own bank loans.

Almost all commercial mortgages will include a **five year call,** also known as a **balloon.** Since it is impossible for a financial institution to know what interest rates will be in future years, they will want to retain the right to adjust the rate on the investor's loan at the end of the fifth year. Although the bank has the right to demand payment in full on the balance of the note at that time, this rarely happens. If the investor has been making timely monthly note payments and there is every indication that his Tenant's business continues to be positive the bank will want to retain the loan in its portfolio.

In a five year call the interest adjustment of the loan may possibly be one to two percent above its current rate. But by the beginning of year six of the Tenant's Lease, chances are that there will have been at least one rent increase. It is also likely that the investor will have paid down a large amount of the interest part of his note over the proceeding five years. So even if the new rate is greater than it was in the previous five years there is an excellent chance that it may have little impact on the investor's overall return.

Some investors will obtain an **adjustable rate mortgage (ARM)** at an interest rate perhaps two percent lower than a loan with a higher fixed rate. Their feeling is that even if (or when) their rates eventually rise the additional income they will have obtained at the lower rate will more than compensate for the rise. This will dramatically increase the return on their investment. But even with a higher interest rate, *the Equity Buildup on their loan coupled with the monthly cash return from their Tenant will give the investor an initial thirteen to fifteen percent return increasing annually.* (For more information on the higher rate of returns with ARMs see Chapter 6: RETURN ON INVESTMENT)

There are some investors who may not need the monthly cash return from their Tenant to supplement an already adequate income and will use that cash to pay down their mortgage each month. In this way they not only save themselves a great deal of interest which is at its highest at the beginning of the loan, they will also have a twenty year note paid off in eight or nine years.

With the security of a monthly assured income from a Credit Tenant and no Landlord expenses or responsibilities, the Net Leased property is considered to be the safest, least labor intensive and certainly one of the most profitable Armchair Investments available.

A Quick Review of Chapter 3

The financing of your Net Lease purchase is perhaps the most critical factor in obtaining the maximum Return On Investment (ROI).

TERMS

Cap Rate – Annual rent divided by the purchase price.

Market Rent – Tenant's average monthly payment per square foot for a similar type of business in a comparable location.

Return On Investment (ROI) – The percentage or monetary return on the investor's cash down payment.

Cash-on-Cash - Annual return on the investor's down payment stated in dollars.

Net Operating Income – The investor's cash return after deducting operating expenses from the annual rent.

Equity Buildup – The steadily increasing "principal" part of the "interest and principal" in a monthly bank payment.

Assumable Loan – The balance due of a loan already in place which can be transferred to a new buyer.

Five Year Call (Balloon) – The bank's right to adjust the interest rate on a mortgage at the end of its fifth year.

Adjustable Rate Mortgage (ARM) – A bank loan which can be adjusted upward by a stated amount over the loan period.

4

NET LEASE vs RESIDENTIAL

Although the purchase of commercial Net Leased properties is not a new strategy, many real estate investors have not been aware of its existence. The traditional route to accumulating wealth through real estate has been to find and convert low-priced distressed residential properties into income producing rental units, being deeply involved in every phase of property management from do-it-yourself repairs to rent collection. However, for the "entry level" investor in real estate who may have very little cash available for the purchase and refurbishing of a rental property, and with a minimum down payment (or possibly no down payment) this may be the only way to begin.

Dozens of excellent books have been written to provide information regarding rental property investments —- their financing, fix-up, and the eventual accumulation of multiple units. But at a certain point, the successful real estate investor may have enough equity in his portfolio to "cash out" and move up to a less stressful, time consuming and labor intensive route to retirement.

This can be accomplished with an initial Net Lease investment, and over time, through tax-deferred exchanges, to the ownership of more and more valuable income producing properties.

In this chapter we define the Net Leased property and show how it differs from investing in residential real estate. To illustrate, we will compare the investment in a Rental Property to one in a Net Lease:

Rental: You own the land and the building.
Net Leased: You own the land and the building.

Rental: You are the Landlord.
Net Leased: You are the Landlord.

Rental: You are the employee.
Net Leased: You have no employees.

Rental: You refurbish the property, find tenants, collect rents, pay property taxes, insurance premiums, and are responsible for all the maintenance.
Net Leased: Your building is in excellent shape when you purchase the property and your Tenant is in place for the length of the Lease. He pays the taxes, the insurance and does all of the maintenance.

Rental: Your income is subject to vacancies, economic conditions, competition, etc.

Net Leased: You will have no vacancies and your net
              income is a rent check each month from
              an "investment grade" Tenant with a
              proven track record, longevity and a
              Lease guaranteeing you a fixed annual
              income for the length of the Lease plus
              option periods. In addition, there are
              periodic rent increases.

Rental: Your financing is usually from your own
              savings plus a note based on the value of
              the property.

Net Leased: Your ability to borrow to purchase the
              property will be influenced by the finan-
              cial standing of your Tenant and the
              terms of your lease.

To summarize: A Net Leased property is an investment in which one owns real estate (land and building)
and leases the building to a single Tenant for a 10 to 25
year initial term. The Tenant, usually a major well-known
retail chain or corporation (a "Credit Tenant") seeking to
take the large amount of debt involved in ownership of
real estate off its books, agrees to occupy the property,
operate its business on the premises, and pay the
Landlord, in addition to monthly rent, all the property's
operating expenses for the length of the Lease. *The
investor's sole duty aside from his payment of the mortgage is
to deposit his monthly rent check.*

There is usually an opportunity for the rent to increase

over time ("rent bumps") as a hedge against inflation, as well as options to extend the Lease beyond its primary term. *Since the Landlord owns both the land and the improvement, the Net Leased property is always a free-standing building.*

This type of real estate investment is passive, similar to owning stock in General Motors, except that the investor receives a guaranteed rent payment as his monthly dividend and is not affected by the overall economic conditions and other factors which make trading in stocks, bonds and mutual funds so precarious.

Further, the commercial Tenant is a positive renter. Unlike residential or apartment dwellers who often abuse the property and then move out, leaving the owner to refurbish and find new renters, commercial Tenants have a vested business interest in seeing that their location is well maintained and attractive to customers. As a result, there is an economic incentive to enhance the owner's property over time.

In this chapter we have outlined the many advantages to owning a commercial Net Leased property:

- The monthly Lease agreement provides a very predictable, long-term income to the property owner.
- Since there are no expenses to be deducted from the monthly rent the income stream is not impacted by future increases in property taxes, insurance premiums or maintenance costs.

- Because of the credit worthiness of the Tenant and the terms and conditions of the Lease agreement the investor can not only enjoy a high degree of security, but will have additional income over time as the inflation hedge feature of the Lease agreement (the "rent bumps") comes into play.

All of these plus the total absence of any involvement in either property management or the Tenant's business affairs make the purchase of a Net Leased property truly an Armchair Investment.

A Quick Review of Chapter 4

A Net Leased property is defined as one in which the investor owns the land and its improvements (a free-standing building) and his Tenant pays all taxes and insurance and does all the maintenance. In addition to the monthly rent the Lease specifies periodic rent increases over time as a hedge against inflation. The investor's sole duty aside from his payment of the mortgage is to deposit his monthly rent check.

Some of the other advantages in the ownership of Net Leased properties compared to that of rental units are:

- No need for property managers or employees.

- There are no vacancies.

- The investor is guaranteed a fixed annual income for the length of the Lease along with periodic rent increases which are negotiated in advance.

- The annual income is not impacted by future increases in property taxes, insurance premiums or maintenance costs.

- There is no involvement in the Tenant's personal or business affairs.

THE BIG THREE

In previous chapters we have presented an overall view of Net Lease investing and a discussion of Lease types, financial terms and advantages of Commercial Net Lease investments compared to those in residential real estate. This chapter addresses three of the most important topics of all: Available properties, their prices, and their locations.

Most investors prefer to choose a property within easy driving distance from their residence. Although with a Triple Net Lease there are no day-to-day (or even month-to-month) management responsibilities, they would still like to be able to visit their investment property occasionally if only for the peace of mind that comes with knowing that it is being carefully maintained and that their Tenant's business is prospering.

But by limiting their choices to those properties within a hundred mile radius of their home (or less) they also greatly reduce the number of properties available in their price range. Although this is a trade-off many are willing to accept, they may have a long wait until a Net Leased property in their target area becomes available. If they have a short-term window (cash now available; a 1031 Exchange deadline) to find the best investment with the largest possible return, they may need to increase their choices to a region rather than to a state.

Before examining the many types of Net Leased properties available and specific examples of the Tenants within each category we must first note that not all Net Leased properties are Triple Net. Many are Double Net, meaning that although the Tenant pays the taxes and insurance, the Landlord is responsible for some elements of the property's upkeep; the most common being for the building's structural integrity (roof, foundation and outside walls). Other obligations may include the parking area, heating and air conditioning systems (HVAC) and possibly other types of repairs. This is most often seen in Leases of those properties valued at less than one million dollars.

Although a Triple Net Lease is the most favorable for the investor, Double Nets should not be rejected before first determining if the Landlord's obligations will potentially be so great as to fatally impact what may still be an excellent investment opportunity. A new or recently constructed building may be in excellent shape; it may also have long-term warranties on the roof and HVAC systems. There is also a "due diligence" period, usually at least thirty days after the Offer to Purchase Agreement is accepted by the seller, for the buyer to evaluate the condition of the building.

Even with a Triple Net Lease it is prudent to have a competent structural engineer check the building for present flaws or possible future problems. And it is always possible to negotiate in the Purchase Offer that any problems found must be corrected before the close of escrow. So if there is an excellent "investment grade" Tenant in place, the CAP Rate, length of the Lease and rent bumps are satisfactory and the price is right, a Double Net can still be an excellent investment. (See Part II for a further discussion of Double Nets).

Net Leased properties become available to investors in a number of ways. Three of the most common are:

1) A large corporation or retail chain will have a building custom built in its "signature" style (Taco Bell, Circuit City, KFC, etc.) in a prime commercial location. It will then execute a "Sale and Leaseback" agreement with the builder who will retain ownership of the land and building and either immediately put it on the market, or keep the property for one year, and then sell it in the second year for a long-term capital gain.

2) Real Estate Investment Trusts (REITs), similar to mutual funds, with hundreds of millions of dollars available to invest, will purchase whole chains of commercial properties (restaurants, convenience stores, etc.) with Triple Net Leases in place. They will often keep some and then "flip" the rest for a higher price, placing them for sale with the large real estate bro-

kerages located in various cities throughout the U.S. that specialize in Net Leased properties. These brokers, in turn, make them available through their Brokers' Networks on a split-commission basis to commercial real estate companies that will offer them to investor/clients in their area.

3) Individual owners of Net Leased properties may want to "cash out" for various reasons (retirement, estate settlements, need for cash, etc.). Or they may be ready to trade up to a larger property using their present one in a Tax-Deferred Exchange. They, too, will place them with a commercial real estate brokerage which will in turn make them available to investors.

It is important to note that a commercial Net Leased property can only be a free-standing building with a single Tenant committed to occupying the property for the duration of the Lease. Apartment houses and office buildings obviously do not fit this pattern. Occasionally Single-Tenant office buildings occupied by, for example, large national insurance companies may become available as Triple Nets, but these are rare.

Industrial buildings and office/warehouses with long-term Triple Net Leases to local or national credit tenants can also be excellent investments. You will occasionally find properties occupied by large corporate and industrial giants such as Airborne Express, Corporate Express, FedEx, UPS, General Electric and Monsanto available as a Triple Net. They can be an excellent purchase for the investor looking for a "high ticket" property.

Other examples of Net Leased properties include:

Convenience Stores
Circle K, Citgo, Conoco Phillips, Golden Gallon, Pantry Store, Philips 66

Day Cares
Kindercare, La Petite Academy, Sunshine House

General Merchandise and Retail Chains
Dollar General, Family Dollar, Fred's, Home Depot, K-Mart, Kohl's, Lowe's, Pier 1 Imports, Sam's Club, Tractor Supply, Wal-Mart

Restaurants and Fast Food Chains
Applebee's, Arby's, Back Yard Burgers, Benihana, Bennigans, Blimpie, Bojangles, Buffalo Wild Wings, Captain D's, Checkers, Chili's, Chuck-E-Cheese, Dairy Queen, Duncan Donuts, Golden Corral, Hardee's, Hooter's, Huddle House, IHOP, Jack in the Box, KFC, Krispy Kreme, Logan's Roadhouse, Long John Silver's, McDonalds, O'Charley's, Pizza Hut, Schlotzsky's, Shoney's, Sonic, Steak 'n Shake, Starbucks, Sweet Tomatoes, Taco Bell, TGI Friday's, Waffle House, Wendy's, Zaxby's

Specialty Merchandising Chains
Auto Zone, Advanced Auto Parts, Bed Bath and

Beyond, Best Buy, Blockbuster Video, Borders Books, Carmax, Cingular Wireless, Circuit City, Foot Locker, Gander Mountain, Hi Fi Buys, Hobby Lobby, Hollywood Video, Jiffy Lube, Movie Gallery, National Tire & Battery, Office Depot, Office Max, Payless Shoe Source, Petco, Petsmart, Radio Shack, Sherwin-Williams, Tires Plus, Verizon Wireless.

U.S. Government
U.S. Post Office, Social Security Administration

Any of the above properties would be excellent investments as long as they meet **The Four Cardinal Rules for Investing in Triple Nets:**

1) An excellent location.
2) A sound, well-constructed building.
3) Occupancy by a strong credit tenant with a long history of business stability and positive earnings.
4) A Lease guaranteed by the corporation, not a franchisee.

The properties most in demand by investors are the restaurant chains. Reason? There are more of them to choose from than any other class of investment and there are a large variety of purchase prices to fit any investment "budget." They also satisfy all the above Cardinal Rules, but especially #1 —- location, location, location.

Restaurants invariably are on heavily trafficked streets close to large populated areas. They may be on an "outparcel" of a large mall and close to other businesses that attract shoppers —- and diners. They could also be located in what are known as "Shadow Anchored Centers." These are properties located within a large parking lot area on a parcel (also known as a "pad") with a Super Wal-Mart or Sam's just across the way to draw customers. But keep in mind that to be a Triple Net they must be free-standing and not part of a Strip Center.

Any of the above scenarios will provide an excellent safety factor to the purchaser. In addition, if the Tenant chooses not to renew the Lease at its termination (or, at worst, goes out of business) the investor still has a building in an excellent business location, easily refurbished (normally at the expense of the incoming Tenant), which he can lease to another restaurant or retailer. Also, by carefully choosing a property leased by a large, successful chain, the buyer can be reasonably certain that his Tenant will continue to operate in that location for at least the duration of the primary lease and will probably continue through the option periods and beyond. If he is doing a good business at that location why would he want to move elsewhere?

Although each of the above categories of investments has its own unique quality, the same general principles of location, quality Tenant, corporate-guaranteed Lease and well-constructed building apply equally to all of them.

The average price for Triple Net properties can vary widely, but it is possible to make some generalizations.

The least expensive, starting at about $350,000, can be found in a number of retail, restaurant and fast-food chains. Some examples:

$350,000 to One Million Dollars

Advanced Auto, Arby's, Blimpie's, Blockbuster Video, Captain D's, Circle K, Dairy Queen, Denny's, Dollar General, Family Dollar, Fred's, Golden Gallon, Hardee's, Movie Gallery, Pizza Hut, Radio Shack, Shoney's, Starbucks, Verizon.

Between One to Two Million Dollars

Auto Zone, Back Yard Burgers, Bojangles, Burger King, Chili's, Circle K, Golden Corral, Hooter's, IHOP, Jack in the Box, Jiffy Lube, Kindercare, La Petite, Logan's Roadhouse, O'Charley's, Sherwin-Williams, Sonic, Taco Bell, Wendy's

Between Two to Four Million Dollars

Applebee's, Buffalo Wild Wings, CVS, Eckerd's, Krispy Kreme, National Tire & Battery, Office Depot, Office Max, Rite Aid, Steak 'n Shake, TGI Friday's, Tractor Supply, Walgreen's

Above Four Million Dollars

A&P, Best Buy, Border's Books, Carmax, Circuit City, Gander Mountain, Kohl's, Lowe's, Sam's Club, Wal-Mart

The above list will give you a general idea of the current range of prices of most of the available Net Leased properties. With your investment "budget" in mind, it is just a matter of choosing the one that will meet the Big Three Goals for investing in Net Leased Commercial Properties: finding the *Right Kind* in the *Right Place* and at the *Right Price!*

A Quick Review of Chapter 5

For a larger selection of Net Leased properties investors may need to widen their target area to a region rather than to a specific city or state.

Double Net properties can be excellent investments if they are new or recently built, have long-term warranties on the roof and HVAC system and are carefully inspected for present flaws or possible future problems.

Properties become available through sales by their builders, REITs or individual owners wanting to "cash out" or trade up in a 1031 Exchange.

A Net Leased property can only be a *free-standing building* with a *single Tenant* committed to occupying the property for the duration of the Lease.

Available Net Leased properties include those occupied by large industrial giants, convenience stores, day cares, general merchandise and retail chains, restaurants, specialty merchandising chains and the U.S. Government.

The Four Cardinal Rules for investing in Triple Nets are:
1) An excellent location,
2) A sound, well-constructed building,
3) Occupancy by a strong credit Tenant,
4) A corporate-guaranteed Lease.

Restaurants are the properties most in demand by investors because they offer a variety of prices and are invariably in excellent locations.

Prices for Net Leased properties start at not less than $350,000.

The Big Three Goals for investing in Net Leased Commercial properties are: Finding the *Right Kind* in the *Right Place* and at the *Right Price*.

6

RETURN ON INVESTMENT

In Chapter 3 (Financing 101) we listed the most important financial terms associated with Net Lease investing. Among them were **CAP Rate**, the percentage   return on an initial cash down payment, and **Equity Buildup**, the "principal" part of the "interest and principal" in a monthly mortgage payment. The combination of these two plus the terms of your loan will determine the **ROI** —- the Return on Investment

If you were to purchase a Net Leased property for all cash, the CAP Rate would be your total return, similar to the purchase of a bank CD or government bond with a locked-in rate. But by leveraging your available cash with a partial down-payment and borrowing the balance, you not only conserve your available funds but also greatly increase the return on your investment through its Equity Buildup.

You will also be able to purchase a much more valuable property which, in addition to producing a greater cash return, you will own free and clear when your note is paid off. *With the monthly rent check your Tenant is not only providing you an excellent cash flow but is also buying the property for you by furnishing the funds for your note payment and its Equity Buildup.*

CAP Rates currently average seven to eight percent on most Net Leased properties, although they can vary from five to ten percent depending on a number of factors:

1) **Supply and Demand**. There are more investors seeking desirable Triple Nets than there are properties available. This has created a "seller's market" that remains relatively constant.

2) **The Rent Payment**. Tenants choose to pay no more than the amount necessary to induce investors to purchase their property. Since *annual rent divided by purchase price equals the CAP Rate*, the lower the rent, the lower the CAP.

3) **Length of the Lease.** When there are only a few years left on the Primary Lease Term the CAP Rate will usually be higher to compensate the potential buyer for his risk that at its termination the Tenant may not choose to continue in business at that location. The seller therefore, to find a buyer, will need to lower the purchase price, thus raising the CAP Rate.

4) **Quality of the Tenant.** Purchase of a Walgreen Drug, Wal-Mart, General Electric or a Circuit City would be comparable to investing in AAA rated bonds with just about zero risk of default. These

companies know they can attract buyers with a lower than average CAP Rate.

In addition to the CAP Rate and the Equity Buildup, we next need to consider the third element in calculating the Return on Investment: The Loan. There are two basic loan types: a **Fixed Rate Mortgage** and an **Adjustable Rate Mortgage (ARM)**.

Many investors feel more comfortable with a predictable fixed-rate loan. Although its monthly payment may be calculated on a 15 or 20 year term it will usually include a **"five-year call"** (also called a **"balloon"**), meaning that the bank retains the option to adjust the interest after the fifth year. However, this adjustment usually will not significantly impact the overall return on an investment for two reasons:

1) The new rate probably will not differ greatly from the present one, increasing at the most perhaps one to one and a half percent.
2) By year six the rent bumps in the Lease will have come into play and between the Equity Buildup and the interest paid down on the note the overall return will probably be at least equal to its initial rate.

Other investors may opt for a lower interest ARM. This loan usually will contain a cap on its annual percentage rise as well as an overall cap on the total interest adjustment over the loan period. *The difference in the percentage return to the investor between a 4% ARM and a*

6.5% fixed-rate loan can be considerable. To illustrate, we will assume the purchase of a Net Leased property for One Million dollars with 20% down and these numbers:

Purchase Price $1,000,000
Down Payment 200,000 (20%)
Bank Loan, 20 year term 800,000 (80%)
Annual NOI (Rent) . . . . 80,000 (8 CAP)
Monthly Rent Payment 6,667

The first year cash return on the down-payment and the total return including the Equity Buildup at varying interest rates would be as follows:

Interest Rate	Cash Return on Down-Payment	1st Yr. Total Return Cash + Equity Buildup
4%	10.91%	24.24%
4.5%	9.63%	22.26%
5%	8.32%	20.27%
5.5%	6.9%	18.28%
6%	5.61%	16.29%
6.5%	4.2%	14.29%

This clearly illustrates the necessity of obtaining the lowest possible interest rate as well as the importance of the Equity Buildup in achieving the maximum Return on Investment.

Note that the above table shows the total return for only the first year. The ROI will continue to increase annually as the "interest" portion of the note decreases and the "principal" portion increases. By year fifteen the

ROI could be a 40% gain (or more) on the investor's down-payment.

Here are two easy to use formulas that will help you to calculate the Cash on Cash and the Total Percentage Return on any potential Net Lease investment. You will first need to run an Amortization Schedule to find the Monthly Note Payment and the first year Equity Buildup. To do this, log on to your favorite Internet Search Engine and enter the words "Amortization Schedule." When you locate a site that contains an Amortization Calculator enter the following information:

- Loan Amount (Purchase price less down payment)
- Interest Rate
- Loan Term (in years)

The Calculator will then supply the numbers you will need to complete the two formulas..

Here's the formula for the cash portion of your ROI:
1) Annual Rent Payment divided by 12 *equals*
2) Monthly Rent Payment *minus*
3) Monthly Note Payment *which equals*
4) Monthly Profit times 12 *equals*
5) Annual Profit *divided by your*
6) Down Payment *equals*
7) **Annual Percentage Return**

Using our Million Dollar purchase with a 20-year term and a 5% interest rate, the Amortization Schedule indicated a monthly note payment of $5,279.65 and a first year equity return of $23,899. With these numbers plus some simple math we can now use the two worksheet formulas to calculate the total Return On Investment.

Cash Return Calculation ($1,000,000 purchase)

1) $ 80,000   (Annual Rent) divided by 12 *equals*
2)   6,667   (Monthly Rent) *minus*
3)   5,279   (Monthly Note Payment) *equals*
4)   1,387   (Monthly Profit) times 12 *equals*
5)   16,648   (Annual Cash on Cash) *divided by*
6) 200,000   (Down Payment) *equals*
7) **8.23% The Annual Cash Return on Investment**

Next we calculate the Equity Buildup:

Equity Buildup Formula

1) Annual Cash On Cash (from #5 above) *plus*
2) 1st Year Equity Return (from Amortization) *equals*
3) Total Return *divided by*
4) Down Payment *equals*
5) **Percentage Total Return (Cash + Equity)**

Again, using our $1,000,000 example, the numbers are

1) $ 16,648   Annual Cash on Cash (#5 above) *plus*
2)   23,899   1st year equity (from Schedule) *equals*
3)   40,547   Total Return (Cash + Equity) divided by
4) 200,000   Down Payment *equals*
5) **20.27% —- The first year Return on Investment**

We will further discuss loan types, sources and strategies in Chapter 8 (Financing Your Purchase), but now that you know how to calculate your Return on Investment you are ready for the next step: *Finding and purchasing your Armchair Property.*

A Quick Review of Chapter 6

The combination of the CAP Rate and the Equity Buildup plus the terms of the loan determine the ROI — the Return on Investment.

With the monthly rent payment the Tenant is buying the property for the investor by furnishing the funds for the Note Payment and its Equity Buildup.

Factors which determine the CAP Rate are:
- Supply and Demand.
- The Tenant's rent payment.
- The number of years remaining on the Primary Lease.
- The quality of the Tenant.

Basic loan types are the Fixed Rate and the Adjustable Rate Mortgage (ARM). Although they both contain interest increases over time, these adjustments usually will not significantly impact the overall Return on Investment because of the Tenant's rent increases and the pay-down of the interest portion of the mortgage.

It is vital to obtain the lowest possible interest rate to achieve the maximum Return on Investment since the difference in the percentage return between, for example, a 4% ARM and a 6.5% fixed rate loan can be considerable.

READY TO BUY?

Consider this scenario: You have funds available and are seriously considering the purchase of a Net Leased property. You've read the first six chapters of this book and you know the advantages of Net Lease over other kinds of investments *(Chapter 1: The Overview).* You also know about the types of Leases *(Chapter 2: They Define Your Return)* and will settle for nothing less than a Triple Net. You're familiar with financing terminology *(Chapter 3: Financing 101)* so you're ready to talk to a lender. If you own management and labor-intensive rental properties *(Chapter 4: Net Lease vs Residential)* you're ready for a rest!

You know the major categories of Net Leased properties, their prices, why they are available *(Chapter 5: The Big Three)* and how to choose them *(The Four Cardinal Rules).* And you can calculate your Return on Investment *(Chapter 6: Cash Return and Equity Buildup Formulas).* So you're now ready for the next step —

finding your Net Leased Armchair Property. How do you find it? Preferably with the help of an experienced, knowledgeable commercial broker. These agents are a different breed from the residential Realtors who are experts in helping you to locate and purchase a home or rental property.

Commercial brokerages specialize in listing, leasing, servicing, and selling many different types of properties: office buildings, industrial and warehouse facilities, shopping centers, vacant land, etc Some also have auction and property management divisions. However, very few specialize exclusively in Net Lease investments. In each major city there may be only a limited number that have expertise in this field and have built up contacts with the large brokerages throughout the U.S. that have Net Leased properties for sale. So how do you find them? Two ways: by telephone or by computer. You might first try the phone.

If you're in a major metropolitan area you will see dozens of brokerages listed in the Yellow Pages under "Commercial Real Estate." In a less populated area there may be very few, if any. In that case you will need access to a phone book from your nearest large city. When you have made a phone connection with a commercial agent here are some suggestions for questions you might ask (in any order):

- *"Does your company specialize in the sale of Net Leased properties?"*

- *"What properties have you recently sold, and at what price?"*
- *"What are the current CAP Rates?"*
- *"Do you have a list of available properties you could send me?"*
- *"Could you find me a property anywhere in the U.S.?"*
- *"How long have you been working with Net Lease investors?"*
- *"Have you coordinated 1031 Exchanges?"*

The phone response to these questions should quickly indicate that agent's level of expertise in this field. Unless you feel reasonably certain you are speaking with someone experienced in commercial Net Leased investments you may want to just thank him for his time and dial the next number.

But if you have gone through the list of commercial agencies in the phone book and still have not found one you feel comfortable with, your next step might be to try the Internet. There you will find a large number of sites devoted to all aspects of commercial real estate. You will also find some companies that list and sell Net Leased properties and have experienced, knowledgeable agents.

However, keep in mind that you will probably be informed about only those properties which are listed by that agency, not the full spectrum of Triple Net properties that may be currently available in your area and throughout the U.S. Also remember that they will be representing not you, the Buyer, but their client, the Seller.

There are also many large commercial brokerages that do not put their listings on the Internet since they prefer not to deal directly with buyers. They may have excellent Net Leased properties available but are accessible only by direct contact through their network of select commercial agents.

So if you are ready for your Armchair Investment but have not found a local commercial Net Lease specialist and your Internet searches have been unproductive, then what? At that point please feel free to contact this book's author. You will find a bio and contact information at the end of this book on page 169 ("About the Author").

Through my brokerage, Commercial Investment Associates, in Hendersonville, Tennessee (a suburb of Nashville) I have located and sold many excellent Net Leased properties to investors from all over the U.S. Many of them I have yet to meet in person. We communicate by phone, fax and E-mail. I regularly hold Net Lease Workshops with both large groups and individuals. My goal: To give my prospective investors the information they will need to understand the principles and details involved in Net Leased investing and to decide if it is right for them. And after that, if they choose, I work closely with them to help them find "The Big Three" — - the *Right Kind* in the *Right Place* and at the *Right Price!* I would be delighted to hear from you.

A Quick Review of Chapter 7

Very few commercial brokerages specialize exclusively in Net Leased properties.

The two ways to locate a Net Lease specialist are by phone (the Yellow Pages) and by computer (The Internet).

Brokerages advertising on the Internet may have a variety of Net Leased properties available, but although they coordinate sales to Buyers they are primarily obligated to their clients, the Sellers.

Many commercial agencies specializing in Net Leased properties choose not to deal directly with buyers but prefer to work only with select commercial brokers.

If you have not been able to locate a commercial Net Lease specialist in your area and your Internet searches have been unproductive, this book's author is available to help you to locate and purchase your Armchair Investment.

THE LETTER OF INTENT

I regularly network with many of the commercial agents throughout the U.S. who sell Net Leased properties. Each has his own method of finding them and working with his investor/clients. In this chapter I will discuss the procedures I follow in my own brokerage, Commercial Investment Associates.

Over a number of years I have built up close relationships with many of the large commercial agencies throughout the U.S. that specialize in obtaining Net Leased properties. I log onto their web sites daily to discover those which have been recently added —- or sold. Many of these brokers also inform me by E-mail of their new offerings. There are also some who regularly alert me to properties that are not included on their web sites but are only made available to select brokers. This is how I locate investment opportunities for my clients. This is my "inventory."

After my review of new properties I choose those

which I will include on the "Available Property" lists I regularly send to my investors. These locations must be occupied by a strong Credit Tenant, have ten years or more left on their primary lease term, and be guaranteed by the parent corporation, not a franchisee. I will recommend only those properties which I, as an investor, would be willing to purchase.

In that my brokerage is located in the Nashville area, many of my clients reside in middle Tennessee. As with most investors, they prefer to be able to drive not more than two to three hours to inspect prospective purchases, either prior to making an offer or within the 30-day Due Diligence period they will have if their offer is accepted.

Approximately every two weeks I forward to my clients (by fax or U.S. mail) a new list of new currently available Net Leased properties in a four-state "target" area: Tennessee, Alabama, Georgia and Kentucky. I also send to many of my local investors —- and to all of my out-of-state clients —- an additional list of properties located in those states or cities outside of this four-state area in which they have expressed a specific interest. The "Currently Available" list contains the following basic information:

- The Tenant
- The Location (city and state)
- Asking Price
- Annual Rent (NOI)
- CAP Rate

- Years left on the primary Lease (the term)
- Rent Bumps (yes or no)

At the bottom of the list I indicate those properties which have especially attractive rent increases and/or include percentage rent. I encourage my clients who see a location of interest on the list to contact me ASAP since the most desirable ones normally do not stay available for more than a few weeks at most. They are sometimes sold in a few days!

When one of my investors contacts me regarding a specific property, I will then provide him with more detailed information regarding the Tenant, the size of the property and age of the building, the street address, the initial date of the Primary Lease and its general terms, the rent increases and their frequency, percentage rent (if any) and the number and length of the option periods.

Since the actual Lease between the present property owner and the Tenant is confidential, it will not be available for inspection at this time. Upon request, I will also do a Financial Analysis of the anticipated purchase. At this point my investor will have the information he will need in order to decide if he would like to make an offer.

If he should choose to proceed, I first check with the listing agent to see if the property is still available. If it is, it is important for the buyer to move quickly, since there may be other investors also ready to acquire that same property. It is not necessary for the purchaser to visit the location at that time. There will be ample opportunity to do that during the 30-day Due Diligence period and time is really of the essence in competing for the most desirable Net Leased properties.

It is also important that the buyer offer, if not full list price, an amount as close to it as possible. While waiting to see if the seller will discount his asking price, another investor who also wants that property may, through his broker, offer full price and thus acquire a property my prospective buyer may wish he had obtained.

The initial offer is made with a simple two-page agreement which I draft for my buyers called the Letter of Intent, usually referred to as an "L-O-I." The LOI is not legally binding on either buyer or seller and there is no earnest money deposit necessary with its submission.

This document is dated and includes the following information: The selling broker's company name and address along with that of the listing broker, identification of the property (the Tenant and the street address), name and address of the prospective buyer, the offering price and its terms (usually all cash at closing), and the amount of the earnest money deposit that will be paid after both the seller's acceptance of the offer and the mutual execution of a Sale and Purchase Agreement.

It will also include the following provisions:

Buyer to have 30 days (the "Due Diligence Period") to:
1) *Inspect and approve of the property.*
2) *Inspect and approve of the Lease.*
3) *Obtain a financing commitment acceptable to the buyer from a lending institution of buyer's choice.*

It also defines who will pay various closing costs (buyer or seller) including transfer taxes, survey, legal fees of each party, the Title Insurance Policy and, in addition, specifies the seller's obligation to provide an Environmental Survey of the property.

It is signed by the buyer and forwarded (usually by fax) to the seller's broker. If the terms and conditions of the LOI are acceptable it will be returned to the buyer with the seller's signature and the date.

The LOI is not legally binding on either party. Therefore, most investors do not think it is necessary to have it reviewed by their attorney before its submission since they may sometimes bid on a number of properties before they finally obtain the one which they will eventually purchase.

However, once the LOI is accepted, it is vital for the purchaser to have, ready to consult, an experienced real estate attorney who will assist with the inspection of the Lease and the analysis and approval of the following document —- *the Purchase and Sale Agreement.*

A Quick Review of Chapter 8

The author's procedure in locating Net Leased properties and communicating with his clients consists of:

1) His ongoing review of new investment opportunities which are listed on specific web sites.
2) Sending to his investors by fax or U.S. mail, approximately every two weeks, a "Currently Available" list of properties that are within easy driving distance from their homes. Only basic information regarding these properties is included.
3) Furnishing more detailed information regarding a specific property upon request.
4) Providing a financial analysis of the prospective purchase if desired.

The buyer will need to offer either full price or an amount close to it if he wishes to obtain the Net Leased property of his choice. He must also move quickly since time is of the essence in competing for the most desirable Triple Nets.

The initial offer to purchase is made with a Letter Of Intent which specifies, in addition to the offered purchase price, some of the legal and financial obligations of both parties. It also includes the buyer's right, during the Due Diligence period, to approve of both the property and the Lease as well as his ability to obtain an acceptable loan commitment.

Once the offer to purchase is accepted by the seller it is vital for the buyer to have an experienced real estate attorney available to assist with the inspection and analysis of the Lease and the Purchase and Sale Agreement.

THE PURCHASE AND SALE AGREEMENT

For the buyer, time is of the essence in bidding for an available property. This is the reason the initial offer to purchase is made with the two-page Letter Of Intent rather than the Purchase and Sale Agreement which requires an earnest money deposit and may contain 15 to 20 pages of legal terminology. The LOI, which simply states the buyer's offering price and basic conditions of sale, can be quickly executed and forwarded by fax to the seller's agent.

If the offer is for less than the full asking price the seller's option is obviously either to accept or to counter. Negotiations can go back and forth until either the buyer withdraws or a final sale price is mutually agreed upon. Often the seller will not immediately respond but will have his agent hold the LOI and wait to see if any better offers materialize. If the offer is substantially below the asking price the seller may not even bother to respond.

When there is an agreed-upon price the next step is

the Purchase and Sale Agreement, usually drafted by the seller's attorney. This document specifies the conditions necessary to protect both parties. In addition to a full legal description of the property it will include (not necessarily in this order):

- *The purchase price; how and to whom it is paid.*
- *The earnest money deposit; where and by whom it will be held and conditions of its return to the buyer.*
- *The buyer's right of entry to inspect the property, and upon approval, his acceptance of the property "as-is."*
- *The buyer's right to terminate the agreement within his 30-day Due Diligence period. Also his right, before closing, to inspect the Title Policy.*
- *Contingencies in the event of destruction or damage to the property before closing.*
- *Buyer's and seller's remedies in the event of default by either party.*
- *Verification of the seller's right to execute the agreement.*
- *The closing costs to be incurred by either party for the Title Insurance Policy, environmental report, survey, transfer taxes and recording fees; also the escrow and attorneys' fees.*
- *A list of the documents that will be forwarded to the buyer after execution of the Purchase Agreement: The Tenant's Lease, a survey of the property, an environmental report and, if available, a recent appraisal report.*
- *The proration of the property tax.*
- *The location of the Escrow Office and a projected date of closing.*

- *The brokers' names, their companies and the amount of their commissions.*
- *The address of legal notice to seller, buyer and buyer's attorney.*
- *The projected date of the buyer's possession of the property.*

The buyer will normally receive the Purchase and Sale Agreement within a week after the LOI is executed by both parties, although it could take much longer if the seller's attorney is too busy to draft it immediately. Some investors have waited two to three weeks before its receipt. If this should happen, the buyer need not be concerned that the deal may have fallen through or that perhaps the seller is considering an offer he may have subsequently received. Although this is possible, since the LOI is not legally binding on either party, it is unlikely.

The buyer's agent will be in constant contact with the seller's agent to obtain an update on the status of the contract and they both will be working together to keep the purchase process moving as smoothly as possible. Once the seller has signed the LOI the listing agent will inform other prospects that there is an agreement on the property but may accept "back-up" offers to be in place in case the purchase should fall through.

The buyer normally will forward the Purchase Agreement to his attorney immediately upon its receipt since in addition to his checking out its terms and conditions, there will often be negotiable items. As an example, in some states it is normal and usual for the seller to pay for the Title Policy; in other states the buyer pays. Most Purchase Agreements will specify that the buyer is to bear this expense. This can add, depending on the value of the property, from several hundred to several thousand dollars to the buyer's costs. His attorney can often negotiate with the seller's attorney to either relieve his client of this expense or perhaps to compromise and have each party pay half; or maybe to agree that the buyer pay only up to a certain amount.

Other negotiable items might be: To change the location of the closing to the buyer's city; or who will bear the cost of a new survey or appraisal; or that the purchase is to be conditional upon specified repairs to be made to the property before the close of Escrow. A copy of the Purchase Agreement should also be sent to the buyer's broker so that he may also examine it and perhaps make suggestions.

There is one other important item usually not noted in the Purchase Agreement: The Tenant will often have a 30-day Right of Refusal to purchase the property in the event of its sale. Although Tenants rarely exercise this right it is a distinct possibility and the buyer normally will not be aware of it until he has received his copy of the Lease. Even if the Tenant has no intention of exercising this option it will be necessary to wait either until the expiration of the 30-day period or the Tenant's notification to the seller that he has waived that right before

Escrow can close.

Since the Lease will not be available for the buyer's inspection until he has signed and returned the Purchase Agreement to the seller with his earnest money deposit, buyers are often uneasy making an offer until they know its full terms and conditions; they will so far have had only the general knowledge conveyed by the listing agent. However, there will be ample opportunity to inspect the Lease during the next phase in the purchase of the Net Leased property: The Due Diligence Period.

A Quick Review of Chapter 9

The initial offer to purchase a Net Leased property is made with a simply-worded Letter Of Intent rather than the more involved Purchase and Sale agreement.

After mutual agreement on a purchase price the seller's attorney will forward to the buyer the Purchase and Sale Agreement which sets forth the conditions and contains the legal terminology necessary to protect both parties.

In addition to checking out the terms and conditions of the Purchase and Sale Agreement, the buyer's attorney will also be involved in the negotiation of other aspects of the purchase.

The Tenant will often have a 30-day Right of Refusal to purchase the Net Leased property in the event of a sale. Although Tenants rarely exercise this right, Escrow cannot close until it has been waived.

Since buyers do not have an opportunity to review the Lease prior to their completion of the Purchase and Sale agreement they are often uneasy in making an offer on the property. However, they will have ample time for its inspection during the Due Diligence period.

10

DUE DILIGENCE

The buyer's 30-day Due Diligence period starts after he has sent a fully executed Purchase Agreement with his Earnest Money deposit to the seller and has in turn received a signed confirmation of its acceptance. In a few days he will receive a "Due Diligence Package" containing the Tenant's Lease, a survey, and a copy of the Phase 1 Report certifying that there are no hazardous materials present on the property.

Within this period, if the buyer is dissatisfied in any way with the property or the Lease, or has not been able to obtain confirmation of an acceptable loan he may then notify the seller in writing that he is withdrawing his offer to purchase. It is not necessary to give a reason. His Earnest Money, held in escrow, will be returned and he will have no further obligation regarding that transaction.

THE PROPERTY INSPECTION

During the Due Diligence period the property inspection is usually the number one priority. As previously noted, since time is of the essence in submitting an offer, it is not necessary to visit the property until there is an agreement on the purchase price. But once a Purchase and Sale Agreement is in place the buyer will need to not only carefully examine the building to see if it has been well maintained and to determine what possible present or future repairs it may require, but also to make inquiries regarding the location.

The local Chamber of Commerce would be a good place to begin; adjacent business owners may also supply additional information; the number of "For Lease" or "For Sale" signs on nearby buildings and the general appearance of the neighborhood should be noted.

If the property is a restaurant or retail establishment, unless specifically requested not to, the buyer may want to talk to the manager. He will be an excellent source of information regarding the volume of business and if the owner is pleased with the location. However, the prospective buyer should be careful to reassure the manager that should the purchase transpire, his relationship with the owner will continue as usual and the only anticipated change will be the destination of the rent check.

If the buyer is satisfied with the location it is usually advisable to have the building inspected by a qualified structural engineer. Even though the purchase may be a Triple Net, with the Tenant responsible for all maintenance and repairs, it will become the buyer's building at closing and he will need to know if there are any construction flaws that might possibly cause future problems. All structural elements, especially the foundation, the outside walls, and the roof, will need his engineer's O.K.

The condition of the landscaping, parking area, and outside lighting should also be observed. A 20-year manufacturer's warranty on the roof and a long-term warranty on the HVAC system might save the new owner a great deal of future expense if the building were to become vacant for any reason. Cracks in the slab of a warehouse may need to be repaired and the parking lot resealed and re-striped. Stained ceiling tiles in an office area would indicate present or past problems. Any significant flaws or signs of poor maintenance noted should be corrected by either the Tenant or the seller before the close of escrow and this obligation needs to be included in the Purchase and Sale Agreement.

THE LOAN

During this 30-day period the buyer will need to initiate an acceptable loan; its terms and interest rate will be a large factor in obtaining the best possible Return On Investment. He must first decide whether to seek a permanent fixed-rate loan or a lower-interest adjustable one. Banks normally calculate the interest on a permanent loan by the current standing of the Ten-Year Treasury Note plus two percent. This rate can rise and fall dramatically; sometimes within a very short period.

For example, in June of 2003 it was at 3.3%, the lowest it had been in 45 years. By August, just two months later, it had risen to 4.45%; by March of 2004 it had again dropped to 3.83% only to rise to 4.73% in June of that year. Timing a Net Lease purchase to obtain the lowest interest rate is just as impossible as timing the stock market.

The rule is for the investor to treat the loan as he would with any other type of purchase —- shop, shop, shop! When he has obtained his best rate it is important to have the bank lock it in with a written commitment that day since it could take 30 to 45 days for the loan papers to be finalized and by then the rate may have changed upward.

The quest for both the lowest interest rate and the best terms usually begins with the institution where the buyer normally does his banking. There is an excellent reason commercial loan officers are quite receptive to loans on credit tenant properties: if for any reason the borrower should default on his loan payment the bank will have, in the loan agreement, the right to collect the monthly rent check directly from the Tenant.

So this type of loan, doubly secured by not only the buyer's credit but especially that of the Tenant is normally a highly-desired addition to a bank's loan portfolio and will usually be obtained at a more favorable rate than for other types of commercial loans.

After receiving a loan quote from his local bank the buyer should then proceed to check with as many other lending institutions as possible to try to locate one with even better terms. Many investors have found three or four banks bidding for the loan on a credit tenant property. In addition to the interest rate, loan origination fees and closing costs are also negotiable.

Very important: The bank will insist on choosing its own appraiser; this will be the buyer's expense. He must be sure to insist that the appraisal fee be not more than twenty five hundred to three thousand dollars. Many investors, this author included, have been stuck with a five to six thousand dollar appraisal just because they failed to negotiate this item in advance.

Some investors prefer to purchase their Net Leased property with a lower-interest **Adjustable Rate Mortgage (ARM)** rather than a permanent loan. ARMs generally begin with an interest rate that is two to three percent below a comparable fixed-rate mortgage and after an initial period of perhaps three years will change at specified intervals (usually annually) depending on market conditions.

ARMs also have a "lifetime cap", required by law, that will limit the interest charge over the life of the loan. For example, a "3/1 ARM" is fixed at an initial low rate for the first three years, and then adjusts upward annually until it reaches the cap. It will also specify a limit on the amount of the annual adjustment.

The lower initial interest rate of an ARM will make a dramatic difference in the Return On Investment (ROI) over a fixed-rate loan. Many investors feel that this initial extra return will more than make up for the larger note payments during the ARM's later years. By then the buyer will not only have an increased monthly income due to his Tenant's rent bumps, he will also have two excellent options: 1) He can exchange the ARM for a permanent loan by refinancing the note, or 2) He may be ready, with a 1031 Tax-Deferred Exchange, to trade up to a larger and more valuable Armchair Property. As always, the investor's decision on the choice of financing should be made only after consulting with his CPA.

THE LEASE

Next on the Due Diligence agenda is the Tenant's Lease. It may well run to twenty or more pages and should be thoroughly examined by the buyer and his attorney. As discussed in Chapter 2, it defines the conditions of the Tenant's occupancy and contains at least the following provisions (not necessarily in this order):

- *The number of years in the initial (primary) term and its commencement date.*
- *The number and length of the option periods.*
- *The annual rent payment and the time and amount of their increase.*
- *Percentage rent (if any) and its commencement date; the amount and the sales volume "break point" if the percentage doesn't begin in the first year.*
- *The Tenant's obligation for property taxes and insur-*

ance, including a possible penalty if they are not reimbursed to the Landlord within a specified time.

- *The Tenant's responsibility for maintenance, utilities, HVAC, plumbing and electrical.*
- *The Landlord's obligation, in a Double Net Lease, for maintenance and repair of the structural elements of the building.*
- *The identity and location of the Guarantor of the Lease.*
- *The Tenant's termination right (if any) and its details.*
- *Indemnification of the Landlord in the case of injury to persons or property resulting from the Tenant's use and occupancy.*
- *The permitted usage of the property.*
- *The Tenant's right to remove trade fixtures at the termination of the Lease.*
- *The Tenant's requirement to obtain prior written consent of the Landlord before making any structural changes to the building.*
- *The Tenant's right of assignment or subleasing.*
- *The monetary terms and conditions of the Tenant's possible hold over period at the expiration of the Lease.*
- *The Tenant's right in the event of Eminent Domain, condemnation or total destruction of the property.*
- *Applicable penalties if the Tenant is in default or delinquent in the rent payment.*
- *The Lessor's right of periodic inspection of the property.*

- *The Lessor's right to place "For Rent" or "For Sale" signs on the premises during the last 60 days prior to the termination of the Lease.*
- *The Tenant's Right of First Refusal to purchase or lease the property in the event of the building's sale or the termination of the Lease period.*
- *The Tenant's right to install signage on or around the property.*
- *The Tenant's Right of "Quiet Enjoyment", meaning he may occupy the premises without any undue hindrance or molestation from the Landlord.*
- *Events which might constitute the Tenant's default and his remedies to "cure" same.*
- *The Tenant's responsibility for Mechanic's Liens and Personal Property Taxes.*

All of the above, and more, define the rights and responsibilities of both the Tenant and the Landlord for the duration of occupancy of the property and are rarely subject to change since they have been previously agreed upon by both the seller and the Tenant. At the end of the Due Diligence period, if the buyer is completely satisfied with the property and its location, has been able to lock in an acceptable bank loan, and has found no problems with the terms and conditions of the Lease, he will then notify the seller that he is ready to close.

The closing will normally occur within the next thirty days although, with the agreement of both parties, it could be extended if all the paperwork of either the buyer or seller has not yet been completed. Some reasons for this might be that the buyer's loan has not yet been finalized; or the appraiser has not completed his report; or the issuance of the Title Policy has been delayed.

The location of the closing office may be in a city other than that in which the property is located; it may also be in a city in which neither the buyer or the seller reside. This is not a problem since the attorneys representing each party will be in contact with each other by phone and all closing papers can be signed and forwarded to the Escrow officer by fax or mail.

At closing, funds will be transferred by wire from the buyer's bank to the seller's account and the brokers will receive their commissions by check or wire from their respective client's attorneys. The current month's rent will be prorated to the date of closing and credited to the buyer's account; thereafter he will receive his monthly rent check directly from his Tenant. The ending of the purchase process marks the beginning of the buyer's Armchair Investment.

A Quick Review of Chapter 10

Within the 30-day Due Diligence period, if the buyer is dissatisfied with the property or the Lease or has not been able to secure an acceptable loan he may notify the seller that he is withdrawing his Offer to Purchase and his earnest money deposit will be returned.

Inspection of the property and its location is usually the number one priority during the Due Diligence period.

After deciding whether to seek a permanent fixed-rate loan or an ARM, the investor should contact as many financial institutions as possible to obtain the best rate and terms. His loan will be doubly secured since if he should default on his monthly payment the lender will have the right to collect the rent directly from his Tenant.

A very important item in loan negotiations is to limit the appraisal fee.

The provisions of the Lease will define the rights and responsibilities of both the Landlord and the Tenant.

The closing may be in a city other than that in which the investment property is located. Funds will be transferred by wire from the buyer's bank to the seller; the current month's rent will be prorated to the date of closing and credited to the buyer's account. Thereafter the buyer will receive his monthly rent check directly from his Tenant.

PARTNERS

As noted in Chapter 5 (The Big Three) the very least expensive Net Leased properties start at a price of about $350,000. Since most investors pay 20% down and borrow the balance the lowest priced investment will require a minimum down payment of approximately seventy thousand dollars.

To raise this sum, many investors who have over time been purchasing and accumulating rental properties may consider liquidating their holdings and putting the proceeds into a Net Leased property via a 1031 Tax-Deferred Exchange. Others may have this amount available from other sources. However, there are many individuals who have accumulated savings but not enough for the downpayment on a Triple Net.

Their solution has been to join with family members or friends to pool their financial assets and form either a partnership or a real estate investment group, similar to the clubs that invest in the stock market. The three most common methods of accomplishing this are through Partnerships, Limited Partnerships, and Tenants-In-Common.

PARTNERSHIPS AND LLCs

The partnership form of doing business is noted for its simplicity and ease of formation. A General Partnership can be formed with nothing more than a verbal agreement between two or more parties. Nothing has to be filed with state or governmental agencies. The down side is that the partners are jointly and severally liable, meaning that each partner is fully liable for the actions of the other partners.

To reduce the risks and liabilities of a partnership, many investors form a **Limited Liability Company (LLC).** The LLC is a relatively new hybrid form of doing business that combines the characteristics of both a corporate structure and a partnership structure. It is a separate entity like a corporation and therefore carries liability protection for all of its members, but is taxed like a partnership which has the benefit of flow-through taxation. The owners of the LLC are called "members" and can be individuals, corporations, other LLCs, trusts, pension plans, etc.

Most states permit one-member LLCs. A husband and wife are considered two members for formation purposes. The LLC is initiated by filing a form, usually called Articles of Organization, with the local Secretary of State. Most states require that an annual report be filed to keep them apprised of current status, but other than that, there are no other ongoing governmental reports or forms. The LLC is not a tax paying entity; profits and losses flow directly through and are reported on the individual members' tax returns.

Most states require that the LLC have a written Operating Agreement between the members as to how the LLC will be managed and that it contain provisions that will qualify it for beneficial tax treatment. It must be carefully drafted, otherwise the LLC will be taxed as a corporation. As in all real estate transactions, it is important to have the agreement prepared by a qualified, experienced attorney.

LIMITED PARTNERSHIPS

Limited Partnerships are a way for an individual to invest in real estate without incurring a liability beyond the amount of his investment while still enjoying the benefits of appreciation and tax deductions for the total value of the property. Limited Partnerships allow the "pass through" of all the property's tax benefits to the investors and, unlike corporations, their profits are only taxed once.

It also allows centralization of management through the General Partner who makes all the day-to-day operating decisions, is responsible for paying all bills, determines how much cash to distribute to the Limited Partners versus how much to hold in reserve, maintains the books and records of the partnership, researches and assesses the feasibility of possible sales and purchases, and submits periodic reports to the Limited Partners.

The Limited Partners meet on a regular basis with the General Partner to discuss and approve all prospective purchases, sales and financing, and receive periodic reports from the General Partner regarding the financial condition of the partnership. The Limited and General Partners share any profits from rental income or sales in proportion to their investment and according to the terms of the negotiated Partnership Agreement, but there is usually a financial incentive to the General Partner who may receive, in addition to compensation for his management of the partnership, up to fifty percent of the profits.

The terms of the ownership of the Limited Partnership are set jointly at its formation, and although the General Partner may withdraw with the approval of the Limited Partners, he may also be removed by them if he defaults on the terms of the Partnership Agreement or is grossly negligent in his duties.

One area of concern in this form of group ownership is that individual investors in a Limited Partnership do not take title to the properties purchased by the partnership. The title is always retained by the Limited Partnership entity and its members have rights only to their pro-rata share of the profits. Therefore, a member who wants to withdraw from the Limited Partnership must find someone willing to buy his share at an equitable price —- either one of the other partners or a third party who will then become part of the partnership. If he dies his heirs will have that burden. For these reasons many investors prefer to join together as Tenants-In-Common.

TENANTS –IN-COMMON (TICs)

In a Tenants-In-Common interest multiple investors can get together to purchase a Net Leased property, not as Limited Partners, but as individual owners. Each co-owner receives an individual deed at closing for his own undivided fractional interest in the entire property, and each has the same rights as a single owner. His share of rental income or sale of the property is in proportion to the amount of his investment.

The shares of the individuals in the Tenants-In-Common group are not required to be equal and can be sold, gifted, bequeathed by will or inherited. And just as in the individual ownership of Net Leased properties, the distributions to members of the TIC are tax sheltered through their pro-rata share of the depreciation of the property and the interest payments on the mortgage.

Upon the death of a Tenant-In-Common his interest in the property passes through inheritance and does not divide among the other owners. However, to avoid pos-sible conflicts between the original members of the TIC and heirs or subsequent purchasers, when forming the Tenants-In-Common entity it is usually advised to put into the Agreement the following two requirements:

1. If one member dies or intends to sell his share, it must first be offered to the other members of the TIC at the appraised fair market value before being offered to a third party. If none of the other members of the entity choose to purchase his share, then:

2. Only the original members of the Tenants-In-Common group will have voting rights as to the sale or disposition of the property or its on-going operation. The new member (or members) will participate only in their proportional share of the profits.

As in a Limited Partnership, one member of the Tenants-In-Common entity will normally be responsible for the receipt and deposit of the monthly rent check, the payment of the mortgage note, and the regular distributions of profits to all the members. He will also serve as the Tenant's "contact person" to ensure that the property taxes and insurance premiums are paid on time and that the property continues to be well maintained.

In return, he will usually have some form of compensation for this from the other members —- normally a very nominal amount since in a Net Leased property, being an Armchair Investment with no management responsibilities or on-going expenses, these will be his only duties.

A Quick Review of Chapter 11

Potential Net Lease investors who have not yet accumulated the minimum amount of funds necessary to purchase a Triple Net can join with family or friends to pool their financial assets and form either a General Partnership, Limited Partnership or Tenants-In-Common entity.

A General Partnership can be formed with nothing more than a verbal agreement between two or more parties. However, each partner is fully liable for the actions of the others.

The Limited Liability Company (LLC) carries liability protection for its members like a corporation, but has the benefit of flow-through taxation. It is formed by filing its Articles of Organization with the local Secretary of State.

The Limited Partnership is managed by one of its members, the General Partner, who makes all executive decisions and reports periodically to the Limited Partners regarding the financial condition of the partnership. Title to the properties owned by the partnership is retained by the entity; its members have rights only to their pro-rata share of profits.

In a Tenants-In-Common interest each member receives an individual deed at closing for his pro-rata ownership of the property which can be sold, gifted, bequeathed or inherited. Distributions to the TIC members are tax-sheltered through depreciation and the interest payments on the mortgage.

12

THE 1031 EXCHANGE

The 1031 Exchange, so named because it is Section 1031 of the Internal Revenue Code, has been available to real estate investors since 1921. It started out at that time as a simple direct exchange between two parties, but in 1979, in what is known as the Starker Decision, the IRS approved **"Deferred Exchanges"** which allowed taxpayers to receive "like-kind" properties after they had sold their existing property, rather than requiring a simultaneous exchange. Then, in 2000 the IRS officially sanctioned **"Reverse Exchanges"** where the new property is acquired before the old property is sold.

The reasoning behind the 1031 Exchange is that if one does not cash out of an investment, the economic gain has not been realized in a way that produces the cash to pay the tax on the transaction.

Normally when you sell a property, you must recognize gain or loss in that transaction. If it is a gain, it is subject to taxes —- Federal Capital Gains Tax, potential state income tax and potential depreciation recapture taxes. However IRC 1031 states: *"No gain shall be recognized in the exchange of property held for productive use in trade or business or for investment if such property is exchanged solely for property of like kind."*

The concept is simple:

- In a 1031 Exchange, you exchange Property A for Property B.

- The sale proceeds from A are used to pay for the purchase of B.

- By using a "Qualified Intermediary" to transfer both properties and funds, rather than you doing so directly, your tax liability is deferred.

So instead of selling a property, paying taxes on the gain, and then using the reduced after-tax proceeds to buy other real estate, IRC 1031 allows you to defer the capital gains tax owed. This enables full reinvestment of your sale proceeds. The amount not paid in capital gains tax to federal and state governments creates increased equity in your investment. In effect, you receive an interest-free loan from Uncle Sam in the amount you would have paid in taxes. Although it is often referred to as a "Tax *Free* Exchange" it is, as noted above, a "Tax *Deferred* Exchange." However, as we shall later see, there is a condition in which it can be completely tax free!

The basic premise of the 1031 Exchange is that it allows sellers of real estate held for investment purposes to "trade up" to a more expensive property and defer all federal income taxes to a later date. This allows the taxpayer ("The Exchanger") to keep the earning power of the deferred tax dollars working for him in another investment.

In "trading up" the investor can also add money to an exchange and acquire an even more expensive property than he sold. Or he can increase his debt; but he must always use all the proceeds from the "Relinquished Property" as well. Though it is possible for The Exchanger to use part of the cash from the transaction for other means and use the remaining proceeds to do the exchange, any cash thereby obtained will be subject to taxation. This is known as a "Partial Exchange."

There are strict guidelines to be followed in order to accomplish the 1031 Exchange, and as always, it is important to have the guidance of a qualified, experienced attorney and/or CPA before entering into this type of transaction. All aspects of the investor's unique tax situation need to be evaluated. There may even be times when a Tax Deferred Exchange is not the best option.

Properties exchanged are termed **"Like For Like"** and are *any properties owned but not used for the investor's primary residence.* For example, they can be:

- An apartment building for a shopping center.

- Raw, undeveloped land for an office building or warehouse.
- Single-tenant rental houses for a Net Leased retail or industral property.

In effect, any investment property may be exchanged for any other investment property. What an investor cannot do is trade investment property for a personal residence and vice versa. It is, however, possible to convert a personal residence to investment property by renting it to another party for a period of not less than one year and then exchanging it for investment property.

There are also limitations on the individuals involved in a Tax-Deferred Exchange. A spouse, partnership or multi-member Limited Liability Company may not acquire the replacement property. Capital Gains taxes can be deferred only if all of the cash proceeds from the original property are used to acquire a replacement property and the exchanger ends up with an equal or greater amount of debt on the replacement property.

The only other provision in which 1031 Exchanges don't qualify is for dealers in real estate. This means that if a person or corporation acquires property with the intent of a fast re-sale the transaction won't qualify. (Note: A one year holding period is commonly used as a rule-of-thumb.) The IRS has limited exchanges to those properties held only for productive use in a trade or business or for investment, and thereby excludes those held primarily for sale.

There are a number of other reasons to enter into a 1031 Exchange beside the deferral of Capital Gains tax:

- To exchange one property for a larger one, thereby increasing cash flow and greater earnings potential.
- To exchange one property for several properties, or several properties for one property.
- To increase depreciation for tax-sheltering purposes on a building owned for several years.
- To improve the quality of an investment property.
- To decrease (or better yet, entirely eliminate) management responsibility.
- To relocate to another area of the country. (You can exchange anywhere in the U.S.A.)
- For estate-planning flexibility.

HERE'S HOW IT WORKS

1. You (**"The Exchanger"**) own an investment property you would like to sell (**"The Relinquished Property"**) using the proceeds to buy a larger, or more expensive property.
2. You find a buyer who will purchase your present property for all cash.
3. With the help of your attorney, you find a **Qualified Intermediary** ("The QI", also known as a "Facilitator" or "Accommodator"). *This is a person or corporation specializing in 1031 Exchanges who will hold all proceeds and documents in an escrow-type account throughout the transaction.* Many

Title Companies or their subsidiaries are in the business of serving as Qualified Intermediaries. The QI neither begins nor ends the transaction with any cash or properties. It buys and sells the exchanged properties on behalf of The Exchanger in return for a fee. (Typical fees for his services will average about $500 and up, depending upon the complexity of the exchange). The QI cannot have a fiduciary relationship with the Exchanger and therefore cannot give legal advice, but does consult with the Exchanger's CPA, attorney, broker, financial planner, and lender.

4. You now choose the property you would like to acquire **("The Replacement Property").** It is the QI who receives the funds from the buyer of your property and uses them to purchase your new property. Since you have not, at this point, received any funds, you therefore have no tax obligation.

There is a very specific timetable for all these activities:

- You will have 45 days from the date of closing of your Relinquished Property to identify up to three Replacement Properties to your Qualified Intermediary. (See exceptions below). This is known as **"The Identification Period."**

- You will then have 135 days in which to close on your Replacement Property, giving you a total of 180 days (not six months!) from the date of closing of your Relinquished Property to the closing of your Replacement Property.

- You must not miss your identification and exchange deadlines! *Failure to identify within the 45 day Identification Period or failure to acquire the Replacement Property within the 180 day exchange period will disqualify the entire exchange!* (The IRS is very specific about this —and reputable Intermediaries will not act on back-dated or late identifications.)

- You must close on the Replacement Property before the earlier of (a) 180 days after the transfer of the Relinquished Property, or (b) The due date of your federal income tax return (including extensions) for the year in which the Relinquished Property is transferred.

There are some variations within this timetable

- You can identify more than three properties if their combined fair market value does not exceed twice the fair market value of the Relinquished Property (200% Rule).
- You can identify any number of properties if 95% of the total value of the named properties is acquired within the exchange period (95% Rule).
- Identified properties may be changed, in writing, within the 45 day period.

- New construction may qualify if properly identified. Any costs incurred after the 180-day exchange period will not count as reinvestment of exchange proceeds.

Again, because it is really vital to remember: *To qualify for a complete tax deferral all funds from the Relinquished Property must be used to purchase the Replacement Property.* Any funds received but not utilized in the Exchange (called "boot") will be subject to income tax. Also, any debt on the Replacement Property must be equal to or greater than the debt of the Relinquished Property.

A successful exchange moves up in price and up in equity from the property sold to the property replaced. Also important: You must take title to the new property using the same entity which held the Relinquished one. Maintaining "Continuity of Title" is critical to the Exchange.

You will pay taxes on your Replacement Property only if you eventually sell that asset without doing another exchange. However, you can continue to roll over sold properties into new properties without any tax obligation until you either sell off all your existing properties *or until you die.*

If you hold the exchanged property until death, your heirs will received a "stepped up" basis to fair market value, and the capital gain is never taxed! This means the income taxes that were deferred by you now become permanently tax free to your heirs. This is the ultimate in estate planning!

Although you cannot receive any cash in the exchange without the payment of income tax, it is possible, after you have made the exchange and have taken possession of your new property, to at that time refinance your new property. Since these monies are financed proceeds, they will be tax free and may be used at the investor's discretion. And since they are not considered proceeds from a real estate sale, the investor may not be limited to reinvesting in real estate. However, he should always consult with his tax counsel prior to utilizing this feature.

A **"Reverse Exchange"** is a transaction in which one buys a Replacement Property before selling his existing property. It often occurs when an investor finds an ideal Replacement Property that may not be available at a later date when the Relinquished Property is sold. It involves having a "parking arrangement" in which the purchased property is acquired not by the investor, but by the Qualified Intermediary who, in this transaction is now called the "Exchange Accommodation Titleholder."

He will hold title for up to 180 days, during which the existing property is sold and the proceeds are used to buy the desired property. The time deadlines for Reverse Like-kind Exchanges are the same as in the delayed exchange.

There are, however, a few special problems for The Exchanger in the Reverse Exchange: He must be sure that the Relinquished Property will sell within his 180 day period. Also, the newly acquired property must be paid for "up front", before receiving any cash from the sale of the existing property.

In this situation it would be very helpful if the seller of the acquired property were to agree to a long escrow period of at least 60 to 90 days. That will give the Exchanger extra time to find a buyer for his existing property at an acceptable price. As a rule, most 1031 Exchanges are delayed transactions.

Another important consideration for The Exchanger is that he must work with a commercial agent with a wide range of contacts who will be able to produce a sufficient number and variety of Net Leased replacement properties from which he can choose during the 45 day Identification Period. This is another reason to work with only qualified, experienced brokers who have substantial expertise in property exchanges.

In my brokerage, Commercial Investment Associates, I regularly have a list of 30 to 40 (or more) currently available excellent Net Leased credit tenant properties at a variety of prices and locations. Before entering into a 1031 Exchange the investor should confirm in advance that the broker he is working with can fulfill this requirement.

And incidentally, since The Exchanger may identify up to three properties and choose only the one which he will acquire, the two he rejects will come back on the market. Selling brokers are understandably very unhappy about "tying up" an excellent credit tenant property for thirty or more days in a 1031 Exchange, but they have learned to live with it.

By utilizing the 1031 Exchange you may, over time, keep trading up your initial Armchair Investment into a series of larger and more lucrative Armchair Investments, thereby fulfilling your goal of becoming an Armchair Millionaire!

A Quick Review of Chapter 12

The 1031 Exchange is not a simultaneous exchange of properties between two parties, although this is possible, but a "deferred" exchange in which the IRS allows taxpayers to "trade up" to more expensive "like-kind" properties after they have sold their existing property and to defer all capital gains tax to a later date.

Any investment property may be exchanged for any other investment property.

The Exchange is accomplished through the use of a "Qualified Intermediary", a person or corporation specializing in 1031 Exchanges who holds all proceeds and documents in an escrow-type account throughout the transaction.

There are four entities involved in the Exchange: 1) The Exchanger, who would like to sell his presently owned property; 2) The Buyer, who will purchase that property for all cash; 3) The Qualified Intermediary; 4) The owner of the Replacement Property.

There is a very specific timetable that must be followed: The Exchanger will have 45 days from the closing of the Relinquished Property to identify up to three Replacement Properties. He will then have up to 135 additional days to close on one or more of the Replacement Properties.

To qualify for a complete tax deferral all funds from the Relinquished Property must be used to purchase the Replacement Property. A successful Exchange moves up in price and up in equity from the property replaced.

The Exchanger can continue to roll over sold properties into new properties without any tax obligation until he either sells off all his existing properties or until he dies.

At death his heirs will receive a "stepped up" basis in the properties and the capital gain is never taxed.

A Reverse Exchange is a transaction in which one buys the Replacement Property before selling the existing property.

It is vital for the Exchanger to work with a commercial broker with a wide range of contacts who will be able to produce a sufficient number and variety of potential Replacement Properties from which he can choose during the 45 day Identification Period.

PART TWO

Beyond the Basics

BEYOND THE BASICS

Congratulations! If you have read this book from its beginning to this point you are now in possession of the basic information you will need prior to your purchase of a Net Leased property.

In this section we shall present additional items of interest relating to this subject. Some will be further details on topics already covered while others will contain information not previously presented. I hope you will find them all useful in your quest for the perfect Armchair Investment.

Subjects included in this section are:

Brokers' Commissions
Double Nets and Dollar Stores
Ground Leases and Leaseholds
Hazardous Materials
More about 1031s
Owning Net Leased Properties In Your IRA
The Option to Renew
"Packaged" Tenant-In-Common Offerings
The Purchase Offer – Fast, First and Full Price
REITs
Zero Cash Flow Properties

BROKERS' COMMISSIONS

On residential sales, listing agents normally request a 6% commission from the Seller. When the property is sold they then split that commission 50/50 at closing with the buyer's agent. In commercial sales (industrial properties, raw land, apartment houses, office buildings, retail and shopping centers, etc.) a 10% commission is quite common.

This is not the case in Net Lease transactions. On single-tenant Net Leased properties a typical commission to the listing agent — which he will then split with the selling agent — is usually only 2% of the sale price. For some smaller transactions of approximately one million dollars or less there is sometimes a total commission of 3%.

This reduced commission is just a "fact of life" for brokerages specializing in listing and marketing this type of property, since in order to obtain the right to sell these properties they must agree to give the sellers the largest possible financial return. Lower commissions obviously will return greater profits to their clients. These brokerages will often obtain from just one seller (a REIT or a national restaurant or pharmacy chain, for example) the right to market a package of twenty to thirty or more excellent retail properties in prime locations throughout the U.S.

Since there are more buyers seeking desirable Net

Leased properties than there are properties available, these locations usually sell in a relatively short period time and often with a relatively minimal effort on the part of the selling broker. And since most of them are for high dollar amounts there are rarely complaints from the selling brokers about the reduced commissions.

Many of the large brokerages that exclusively list Net Leased properties maintain and market an extensive nationwide inventory of Net Leased properties and have a direct relationship with the sellers. But because of the national scope of the single tenant Net Leased investment business it is also possible that a number of these same properties may be marketed on more than one web site and by various listing services.

This is one more reason for the investor to develop a relationship with an experienced commercial agent who has a thorough understanding of the nature of the Net Lease industry and can network with a number of the leading brokerages to give his client the widest possible choice of available properties in a wide range of locations and at a variety of prices.

DOUBLE NETS AND DOLLAR STORES

As noted in Chapter 5, THE BIG THREE, not all Net Leased properties are Triple Net. Many excellent ones are Double Net, meaning that while the Tenant pays the taxes and insurance and often contributes to some of the maintenance expenses, it is the Landlord who is obligated to finance any large expenditures involved in the building's upkeep; the most common being for the building's structural integrity —- the roof, foundation and outside walls (not including glass).

The Buyer's other obligations may include the parking area, outside lighting, heating and air conditioning systems (HVAC) and possibly other kinds of repairs. So why do investors choose to purchase Double Net properties? Mainly because they are priced at less than one million dollars; often much, much less.

Some of the most desirable credit tenant properties priced between $350,000 to $600,000 are the Dollar Stores —- Family Dollar, Fred's, Dollar Tree, and the one most favored by investors, Dollar General. While all the major dollar stores have the financial strength to weather even a protracted downturn in the deep-discount sector, it is Dollar General that especially fulfills all the requirements of the cautious Net Lease investor; longevity, stability and location.

A Fortune 500 Company now based in Goodlettsville, Tennessee (a Nashville suburb), the first

Dollar General store opened in Springfield, Kentucky in 1955 with no item priced over one dollar — a brand new concept at the time. Within ten years the company had grown to 255 stores with annual sales of $25 million and by 1976, with almost 300 stores, its annual sales exceeded $100 million!

By 1989 there were over 1300 Dollar General stores in 23 states and by 1996 they had exceeded two billion in annual sales. By 1998 that figure had risen to three billion, five billion by 2000, and six billion by 2002. In 2004 they opened their 7,000th store. As of this writing, it is a chain of almost 8,000 stores in 30 states, primarily (for now) in the southern, eastern, mid-western and some south-western states. They are generally located both in small towns off the radar of giant discounters such as Wal-Mart and lower-income neighborhoods (abut 30% of its total stores) in big cities.

Dollar General normally does not build or own its stores. It works with established general contractors who will purchase the land and erect a free-standing "build-to-suit" store (usually 7,000 to 8,500 square feet) utilizing the company's construction plans. The sites are all well-located on a "main" treet with easy egress/ingress and have standard Dollar General signage.

When construction is completed, Dollar General will assign to the builder a ten-year Lease with an 8 CAP, three five-year options, and rent increases in both year six and in the option periods. In some locations there is also percentage rent. The builder, in turn, will either immediately "flip" the property, or may hold it for one year and then sell it in year two for long-term capital gain.

Some of the typical Lease terms are:
- Dollar General will reimburse the Landlord for all taxes and insurance incurred during tenancy.
- Dollar General will pay $1,500 per year for care and maintenance of the parking lot. (In some Leases only $1,200 per year).
- Dollar General will pay up to $750 per occurrence for repair and/or replacement of minor items. (In some Leases only $500 or less).
- Landlord is responsible for HVAC, lighting, plumbing, structure and roof; also for the cost of repair and/or replacement of major items in excess of $750.

So what makes Dollar General such a good investment? First of all, it is an excellent "entry level" purchase for the investor with less than $100,000 available. And because of the large number of stores and their wide geographical area there are usually a good selection of them available to investors within an easy driving distance.

Although the Landlord's responsibilities may at the first reading of the Lease seem formidable, consider this: A brand-new Dollar General store may have a 20-year manufacturer's roof warranty along with a long-term warranty on the HVAC system. In addition to Dollar General's annual contribution for its care and maintenance, the parking lot will probably not need to be repaved or re-striped for many years.

Also, a new building with well-installed lighting and plumbing is unlikely to need repairs in excess of $750 during the term of the Lease. (Remember my comment in Chapter 5 regarding having a structural engineer check for present flaws or possible future problems prior to closing?)

An excellent strategy, one especially used by new Net Lease investors, has been to purchase a brand-new Dollar General store with the intention of utilizing it for a 1031 Exchange in year three or four after building up equity in the property, paying down some of the interest on the mortgage, and perhaps accumulating more cash.

The strong demand by investors for Dollar Generals makes them relatively easy to sell at that time; especially since there will be a rent increase in year six. Also by then, if there is percentage rent, the store may have reached or be near its break point. But there is also no reason a Dollar General cannot be a permanent investment. There are some investors with large financial resources who *only* buy Dollar Generals, accumulating a portfolio containing five to ten or more.

For the investor with limited financial resources looking for absolute safety in a relatively low-priced Net Leased property, a Dollar General would be hard to beat. But the same principles also apply to the purchase of *any* Double Net property in good condition, a long-term lease with rent bumps and an excellent credit tenant.

GROUND LEASES AND LEASEHOLDS

In addition to a Net Lease purchase in which the investor owns both the land and the building, there are two other types of real estate ownership which can be excellent investments: **Ground Leases** and **Leaseholds**.

Normally a Ground Lease is defined as a long-term Lease of *unimproved* land, but most Ground Leases offered by brokerages which specialize in Net Leased opportunities are already fully improved with a structure and a Tenant in place. The duration of Ground Lease terms is usually between 50 and 99 years, during which time the Lessee occupying the structure pays rent monthly to the land's owner (the Lessor).

Although the Lessee owns the building, the Ground Lease owner retains title to the land throughout the term of the Lease. If, at any time, the Lessee defaults under his agreement, the Lessor can terminate the Lease and will then become the building's owner, free and clear of the Lessee's financing terms.

The Lessee is responsible for all expenses of the structure, including real estate taxes, utilities, maintenance and insurance premiums. Just as in a Net Leased property, it is customary for the Lessor to require rent increases throughout the Lease term – either annually, at specified intervals, or with percentage changes in an index such as the Consumers Price Index. There is often a cap on the possible rent increase. *At the termination of the Ground*

Lease all improvements revert to the Lessor on a free and clear basis.

Would a Ground Lease be a wise purchase for the prospective investor? Yes and No. If the property is located in a well-established commercial area it is logical to assume that its value during the long period of the Ground Lease is bound to rise, perhaps dramatically. For the investor desiring to build a long-term portfolio for inheritance purposes it may be one of the safest and best performing investments possible. And assuming that the Lessee is of the highest credit tenant quality (a Walgreen Drug, FedEx, General Electric, etc.) its safety can be unexcelled.

But because of their extreme safety, the CAP Rates on Ground Leases are normally about two percent lower than those of other types of Net Leased commercial properties. Therefore they may not meet the investor's goals for his required cash return. Also, for tax shelter purposes, there is no depreciation allowance, since the IRS considers that land, unlike structures, does not depreciate.

But with the assurance of a steady income stream for the investor's lifetime (and beyond) and the absolute safety of well-located land ownership, a Ground Lease can be an excellent Armchair Investment.

The other side of the coin is the **Leasehold Estate.** This is an investment in which the buyer is paid rent monthly, has no expense or responsibility, *but does not own either the land or the building.* His investment consists solely in his right to collect rent monthly from his Tenant for the duration of the Lease. At its termination his investment is also terminated.

Because of this the Cap Rate on Leaseholds is often about two percent or more *above* current rates for Net Leased properties. A Leasehold purchase is similar to buying "investment grade" bonds with an excellent return but no residual value.

Usually, in contrast to the Ground Lease investor, the buyer of a Leasehold is someone not particularly concerned with building a long-term portfolio for estate purposes but interested in obtaining the highest possible Return On Investment (ROI) during his lifetime with no landlord expense or responsibility. If his Tenant is of the highest quality and has agreed to an extra long-term Lease with multiple option periods, a Leasehold purchase can be an excellent Armchair Investment.

As an example, recently a Leasehold was offered in one of the "hottest" commercial areas of a large southeastern city. The Tenant, a major national drug store chain, executed a twenty-five year Absolute Triple Net lease with *eight* five-year options, thereby committing to a possible sixty-five year Lease period. Even with a flat rental rate during the primary Lease term and rent increases only in the option periods, this Leasehold was purchased by an investor shortly after it was introduced in the market.

HAZARDOUS MATERIALS

In Chapter 10, DUE DILLIGENCE, I noted that once the buyer has executed and returned his Purchase and Sale Agreement with an earnest money deposit he will shortly thereafter receive a "Due Diligence Package." This will contain, among other items, a copy of the property's **Phase One Report** certifying that there are no hazardous materials present on or around the property. This document is of vital importance to the purchaser of *any* property since, once Title is passed, any hazardous materials that might be found at a later date will obligate a very expensive clean-up by the new owner.

Net Leased properties are normally "clean" types of businesses such as restaurants and fast-food chains, drug stores, grocery chains, or general or specialized merchandise properties. However, there are some excellent national paint stores, automotive repair establishments and convenience stores with gas pumps available as Triple Nets.

Underground gas storage tanks may have at some time in the past been leaking. Oil products or battery acids may have been dumped behind an industrial building. And even the "clean" properties may have been built on an abandoned landfill site.

Usually, before a building permit is issued by a municipality, the builder will be required to have the site inspected by a specialized company, licensed and bonded by the state, that will inspect that site to ascertain that no hazardous materials are present. This is called a "Phase One Investigation" in which soil samples are collected and analyzed to determine if any contaminants may be present.

A title search will also be initiated to see how the location has been used by previous owners. If, as a result of these investigations, no evidence of prior contamination is found, it will be given a "clean bill of health" known as a "Phase One Approval." This is the document that will usually be included in the Due Diligence Package. If it is not, the buyer would be well advised to delay taking title to the property until it is provided.

This is why: If, after the initial investigation, there is any evidence found of contaminants in the soil, the procedure will then move into "**Phase Two**", in which a core sample is drilled and analyzed to determine the extent of the problem. If there is only negligible surface contamination, that soil will be removed and replaced with clean fill. If it is then determined that "there are no further risks posed to public health, welfare and the environment", it is usually given an O.K.

However, if the problem is found to be extensive, involving more than just a simple removal and replacement of the surface soil, the property will then move into "**Phase Three**", a very expensive and time-consuming procedure to thoroughly rid the site of any contamination down to a depth of up to fifteen feet. In addition, it must be re-evaluated every five years! The law states that the current owner of the property bears the responsibility for the clean-up. It is for this reason that the buyer will need the seller of a Net Leased property to produce a Phase One Report before taking title.

MORE ABOUT 1031s

In Chapter 10, THE TAX DEFERRED EXCHANGE, we noted that one of the primary reasons for an exchange is to avoid payment of capital gains tax on the sale of a property held for investment purposes. It may be important, in advance of a decision to enter into an exchange, to determine just how great the prospective savings might be. The reason? It may not be large enough to justify both the expense of the exchange and the careful observance of the IRS rules. So before deciding to exchange an investment property rather than just selling and paying tax on the gain, it may be useful to know just what dollar amount the gain might offer.

Since the gain on a property is the difference between the *net sales price* (the total cash amount received at closing) and the *adjusted basis,* the obvious first step is to calculate the adjusted basis. Here's the formula:

1) Original purchase price of the property PLUS
2. Purchase expenses (commissions, closing fees, finance charges, etc.) PLUS
3. Capital improvements (new roof, HVAC system, major repairs, etc.) MINUS
4. Depreciation taken (more about that coming up) EQUALS
5. Adjusted Basis

An easy way to calculate the amounts for capital improvements and depreciation is to look at your previous tax returns and see what has been deducted annually for these items. Once you have determined your adjusted basis you are now ready to estimate your capital gain with this formula:

1. Anticipated sales price MINUS
2. Selling expenses (commissions, closing costs, etc.) MINUS
3. Adjusted basis EQUALS
4. Capital Gain

But it's not quite that simple. The capital gain has two parts: The *actual gain* and a significant item called *the recapture of depreciation.* Uncle Sam has allowed the investor an annual tax break by letting him deduct the depreciation on his property in addition to the interest payment on his mortgage. Now he wants some of it back!

So you must calculate into the capital gains formula 25% of the depreciation you have previously taken as a *recapture* of that depreciation. And if you have owned your investment property for a considerable length of time, say ten to fifteen years, you may find that figure to also be a considerable *dollar* amount.

You are now ready to estimate your potential tax liability by utilizing the three factors we have noted: The anticipated sales price minus the adjusted basis and the depreciation. Depending on your tax bracket you may consider that for a savings of perhaps less than $5,000 to $10,000 it may not be worthwhile to enter into a 1031

Exchange. Many investment and rental property owners have come to that conclusion after realizing that the dollar value of their properties and the amount of tax saved would not be high enough to justify utilizing the 1031 Exchange as a tax-planning tool.

OWNING NET LEASED PROPERTIES IN YOUR IRA

Very few investors realize that their IRAs can be used to purchase real estate; most believe that their only investment options are bonds, bank CDs, mutual funds or the stock market. Remember, a retirement account (IRA, SEP, Keogh, 401(K), etc.) is not an investment — it is simply an account that *holds* your investments. Most companies that administer retirement accounts aren't set up to handle real estate and therefore have no incentive to inform their customers that real estate is an alternative investment choice.

To purchase real estate in your IRA you must establish a self-directed account (SD/IRA) with a company/custodian that specializes in and is set up to administrate a Real Estate IRA. This can be done by either establishing a new account or rolling over the assets of an existing account. (Be sure there are no surrender charges for rolling over the account).

Your Real Estate IRA can buy and sell any kind of investment property and will be the entity that buys, owns and sells the property —- not you personally. You don't withdraw the money from the IRA to buy the property; the custodian buys the property in the name of your self-directed IRA and rental income is paid not to you, but directly into your IRA.

All expenses and profits from your Net Leased property must flow in and out of your self-directed IRA. (Remember that with a Triple-Net property expenses, if any, will be negligible since there are usually no operating expenses or improvements to be made). However, there are specific guidelines regarding this type of investment:

- Your IRA cannot purchase a property that you, your corporation, partnership or LLC presently own.
- You cannot live or work in a property owned by your IRA.
- If you own rental houses in your IRA, renovation expenses must be paid out of your IRA.
- You may not keep a portion of the funds from a sale of your property. All income generated must return directly to the IRA.
- It is possible to finance a property that is owned by your IRA, but the financing must be "**non-recourse**", *meaning the property, not the IRA account is the sole security for the loan.* (Triple Net properties with excellent credit tenants will most often qualify for this type of loan)
- Your real estate IRA can buy a partial interest in a property through a Limited Partnership or Tenants-In-Common entity, but you must have an "arms length" relationship with your investment property, so it cannot be a property that is used by you or certain family members. Also, your business cannot use or occupy any part of the property.

The process of purchasing real estate with your IRA is very similar to purchasing other conventional investments with your IRA, with very few exceptions. Once your account has been established and properly funded, with the help of your commercial broker, you choose a desirable Net Leased property. Your Custodian will then purchase that property with the funds in your IRA.

He will need the following information: Name and location of the Net Leased property you are purchasing, the amount needed from your account, where the funds are to be sent, and what documents will be required. Your attorney, CPA and/or real estate broker will be able to coordinate all this information for you. Here are some of the rules you must follow:

- **TITLE:** The asset must be titled in your IRA's name and specified to be "For The Benefit (FBO) Of Your Named IRA."
- **FUNDING:** Needed funds must come directly from your IRA. The Custodian sends funds directly to the title company/closing agent/attorney per your instructions. Funds can be remitted by check, cashier's check, or wire.
- **EXPENSES/PROFITS:** Any expense associated with your Net Leased investment, such as mortgage payments, must originate with your IRA. All income generated by your Net Leased property must return to your IRA in order to retain the tax deferred or tax free status of the investment. Once received by the Custodian, the rent checks are

deposited into your account.

- **SIGNATURES:** Documents regarding IRA investments must be signed by the Custodian acting on behalf of your IRA.

When you are ready to sell or exchange a property (Yes, you can also do a 1031 Exchange through your IRA), your attorney will need to request the original documents from your Custodian. This is done by completing a "Sale Direction of Investment" form. Once the property has been sold or exchanged, all funds obtained in a sale or new properties acquired in an exchange will be placed by your Custodian into your IRA.

To conclude: Net Leased commercial properties are perfect for a Real Estate IRA since they meet all of the rules. And because you own them in your IRA, profits are not taxed. Best of all, there is a limit on how much you can contribute each year to your retirement account but there is no limit on how much the account can earn.

For more information on this subject and the names of companies that specialize in and administrate this type of investment and their fees, go to an Internet search engine and put "Self Directed IRAs" in the search box.

THE OPTION TO RENEW

The prospective purchaser of a Net Leased investment will need to approve three important items before closing: the location of the property, the quality of the Tenant, and the terms of the Lease. Prior to his purchase, the Lease will already be in place, and both the new owner and the Tenant are bound by its terms. These will include the annual rent, its increases, the length of the primary Lease term, and the Tenant's Option to Renew.

For the buyer, options are both a favorable provision of the Lease and a necessary evil. Few Tenants will enter into an agreement to occupy a commercial property unless they know in advance that if their business is prospering they will be able to remain at that location beyond the primary Lease term.

They also know that if a different location at some time in the future might be more beneficial to their business, or that "market rent" at option time may be lower than the rent specified in their Lease, they will have three choices: To exercise the option with the terms as stated in the original document, to attempt to renegotiate those terms, or to relocate.

And that, for the investor, is the problem. His obligations under the existing Lease include his acceptance of the Tenant's right to renew at the end of the primary Lease period. But there is no similar requirement that the Tenant must exercise that right.

Since the Option to Renew usually mandates an upward adjustment in the monthly rent, the Tenant may attempt to renegotiate a level rent at that time or even perhaps a lower one in return for his agreement to remain at that location. Although most Tenants exercise their options with the terms as stated in the original Lease, there is always the possibility that this may not occur.

The solution to this potential dilemma for the buyer is, as always, *location, location, location* in choosing his investment property. If his Tenant's business is prospering he will not only have no reason to move elsewhere, he will have every reason to stay.

If the investor has purchased a property in excellent condition in a strong and growing commercial area, and if at option time his Tenant should threaten to leave, he will therefore be confident in his ability to lease his property to another equally good Tenant at the same terms, or perhaps even better ones. Under these circumstances, the lessor will always be in a dominant position in the event of option renegotiations.

This is another example of why, in addition to having a strong credit tenant and an excellent return on his investment, one of the buyer's most critical considerations in the purchase of a Net Leased property is the choice of a prime location for his Armchair Investment.

"PACKAGED" TENANT-IN-COMMON OFFERINGS

In Chapter 11, PARTNERS, we discussed Tenants-In-Common, a strategy in which multiple investors can get together to purchase a Net Leased property as individual owners. The usual procedure in this type of group ownership is to locate a desirable property, find partners, form the TIC, and purchase the property. One member of the Tenants-In-Common group will usually be responsible for the receipt and deposit of the monthly rent check, the payment of the mortgage note, and the regular distribution of profits to all the members.

There is a recent development in the commercial real estate industry which simplifies this process by making available to investors large, expensive properties (up to twenty million dollars or more) and a ready-made TIC group of up to 35 members, each of whom will own a pro-rata share of the property and not only participate in profits but also in the equity build-up and the pass-through of the tax benefits of property ownership.

This new development allows the small to mid-size investor the opportunity to participate in the ownership of commercial-grade "blue-chip" assets which would normally be much too large for individual investors. In addition, it offers the benefits of a Triple Net Lease (passivity and security) while permitting the purchaser to have a better chance to achieve higher overall returns than those obtained in smaller, less significant properties. In commercial property investment, bigger is usually better. It also relieves the investor of the burden of finding compatible Tenants-In-Common partners.

Some examples of recently-offered properties are:

- A senior assisted living center
- Luxury hotel & Water Park
- National Furniture Chain Building
- Corporate Headquarters Building
- Barnes & Noble/Petco Retail Center
- Fully-leased multi-tenant office/warehouse
- Prestige retail power center
- Retail business center —- fully leased

The prices of the above properties range from five million to twenty million dollars and the minimum cost of one pro-rata TIC share ranges from a low of $100,000 to a high of $700,000 with most of the prices somewhere in between.

The sponsoring organization acquires the property, performs any necessary management duties and handles all the paperwork. Financing is already in place, so the purchaser is not involved in obtaining a loan. It is very much like investing in a mutual fund with the added benefit of financial security and property ownership.

This investment will also qualify as a 1031 Exchange property and can be included in an investor's self-directed

IRA. The holding period will fluctuate according to the individual property and its "life expectancy." If an eventual sale or trade is recommended by the Sponsors all individual TIC holders will then have to unanimously agree to the recommended sale. However, minority or dissenting owners can be bought out at fair market value, and as with all Tenants-In-Common properties, each owner's share can be sold, gifted, bequeathed by will or inherited.

There are stringent requirements regarding the net worth of the participants in each offering and each prospective co-owner is an "Accredited Investor" under government regulations. If you are interested in this type of investment please contact this book's author for more complete information. You will find contact information on page 169 ("About the Author").

THE PURCHASE OFFER: FIRST, FAST, AND FULL PRICE

Because there are more investors seeking desirable Triple Nets than there are those available, when a choice property becomes available it is vital for the investor to submit a Letter Of Intent as soon as possible at either the asking price or very close to it. The LOI does not require an earnest money deposit. It simply states the offering price and some essential conditions to be included in the follow-up Purchase and Sale Agreement.

Listing agents will normally contact their sellers the same day an offer has been received from the buyer's broker. If it is for the full asking price it usually becomes a "done deal" at that time. Sometimes the price may be negotiable, and I have represented investors willing to lose the property who have played "hard ball" and gotten a discount from the offering price. I have also had investors who lost a desired property because another buyer, through his own broker, bid sooner and higher. Here are some examples:

I recently found a listing for a large, national electronics chain property in an excellent high-profile location in one of the "hottest" retail areas of Nashville. It was an 8 CAP with a 20-year primary Lease, two five-year options, rent increases and percentage rent. It was also priced fairly at $5.5 million.

I immediately contacted one of my investors who had expressed interest in acquiring a local "high ticket" credit tenant retail property. This was his ideal target purchase! He checked with his partner (an attorney) and called me back with instructions to submit an offer of $5.3 million.

When I told him that, in my opinion, he'd need to bid much closer to the asking price on such a desirable property he said, *"We're willing to pay the full price if we need to, but we want to see if the seller will counter at $100,000 or so less."* As per my instructions, I forwarded the offer to the listing agent. The seller didn't even respond!

When I called the listing agent the next day he confirmed that although the property was still available he'd had a lot of interest in it and suggested that if my investor really wanted the property he'd have to come up to either the list price or a figure close to it. My buyer was out of town for the next two days, and when he returned he instructed me to increase the offer to $5.4 million. I then called the listing agent who informed me the property had been sold the day before at the full $5.5 million price. My buyer was devastated!

Moral: If the price is fair and you really want to be sure to acquire the property don't hesitate to offer full price immediately.

Sometimes a delayed offer still has a happy ending. I found an excellent purchase opportunity for a national chain restaurant, also a high-profile retail location with all the right numbers – cap rate, length of the Lease, rent increases, options, etc. My potential buyer said he wanted it and was going to check out the location and the property the next day to confirm its desirability. Unfortunately, family and business affairs necessitated a delay in his visit for almost a week.

You can imagine the rest of the story. It was gone by then and I had another very unhappy investor. However, I maintain excellent personal relationships with my network of listing agents. They will often contact me when I have submitted a Letter of Intent for properties that were for any reason unavailable at the time and have subsequently come back on the market.

This is why properties sometimes again become available after the buyer's 30-day Due Diligence period:

1. The investor may not have been able to obtain an acceptable loan.
2. After visiting the property, the potential buyer may not be satisfied with the building or its location.
3. Three properties may be identified for a 1031 Exchange. The two that are rejected will come back on the market. (This is the most frequent reason).

The restaurant property's listing agent contacted me as soon as he was notified that his potential buyer was going to "pass" on the purchase. I then called my buyer to confirm that he still wanted the property (he did) and immediately submitted an updated LOI on his behalf.

He is not only delighted with his purchase, but when, six months later, another restaurant in that chain became available at the same terms and conditions, he immediately offered full price! His subsequent visit to the property confirmed that the building and location were excellent and the transaction closed shortly after his Due Diligence period.

REITs

In Chapter 5, THE BIG THREE, we discussed the ways Net Leased properties become available to investors. One common source for Triple Nets is through REITs, Real Estate Investment Trusts, similar to mutual funds with hundred of millions of dollars available to purchase individual or chains of commercial properties.

Many of these REITs (rhymes with "beets") have a management division for the properties they will keep "in house." Other properties they will "flip" and make available to investors through the brokerages throughout the U.S. that specialize in the listing of Net Leased properties.

There are roughly 180 publicly traded REITs available to investors and they work in much the same way as publicly traded stocks in the major stock exchanges. As with most mutual funds, REITs provide an annual report, prospectus and other financial information and their shareholders receive income from their annual dividend distributions.

Many REITs specialize in specific types of commercial properties, such as shopping centers, office buildings, hotels, RV parks, retirement homes, self-storage facilities, industrial or retail properties. To qualify as a REIT under the Internal Revenue Code, they must pay 90% of their taxable income to their shareholders each year. They must also invest at least 75% of their total assets in real estate and generate 75% or more of their gross income from their investments in real property.

Purchasers of shares of a REIT are not buying real estate; they are buying shares of a *company* that buys real estate and is thus susceptible to the same ups and downs of the stock market and management decisions as any other type of mutual fund.

Although historically REITs in general have returned six to seven percent annually to their investors, this income is subject to capital gains tax and has none of the many advantages of a Net Lease investment, such as the tax shelter from depreciation and mortgage interest payments, equity buildup, cash leverage, tax-deferred exchanges and total ownership of real property. And, as with many mutual funds, there are "front end loads", "back end loads", and management fees. The investor also has no control over when his REIT will buy or sell its holdings or how it will be managed.

To illustrate the uncertain returns that may be achieved by those investors who purchase shares in REITs, I quote the following article which appeared on February 10, 2005 in "Loopnet News", a newsletter subscribed to by many commercial brokers who specialize in Net Leased Properties:

"REIT SHARES DROP

Real Estate Investment Trusts are struggling to live up to investor expectations. REIT shares are down 8 percent so far this year. Of 20 companies covered by Credit Suisse First Boston, 13 have given 2005 earnings guidance that is less than or just at analysts' already-modest estimates. The strongest growth is to come from REITs that own malls, in part because of continued strong consumer spending. The office and apartments REITs may prove more challenging. Apartment REITs are issuing much of the disappointing guidance, due to a sluggish job market and low mortgage rates wooing renters to buy."

However, many excellent Net Leased properties which become available to investors are from retail or industrial properties "flipped" by a REIT. Here is one recent example: In the summer of 2004, two hundred forty-seven "major chain" convenience markets with gas pumps in multiple locations throughout the U.S. became available to investors as Net Leased properties.

Most were priced at under one million dollars and were offered by the REIT's brokerage division at a 9 CAP, 20-year Triple Net Lease with regular rent increases during their primary term and in their option periods. Almost all were in prime locations in major metropolitan areas. Not surprisingly, they were all snapped up by individual investors within three weeks of the offering — some within three days! Here's what happened:

The corporation that owned the markets apparently had a pressing need for cash and for that reason sought a buyer who could quickly fulfill that need. Turning to a major REIT, they unloaded all the properties, thereby solving their fiscal crisis. The REIT, one of the largest in the U.S. specializing in retail properties, purchased all two hundred forty-seven markets but "flipped" the properties immediately, and within one month had recouped their total cash outlay.

However, their management wing retained and operated the stores themselves, thereby obtaining the profits from the gas pumps and the market sales. *And it didn't cost them a cent!* Great strategy. A win-win situation for the REIT and for the investors lucky enough (and fast enough) to acquire one of the properties.

ZERO CASH FLOW PROPERTIES

Most investors will purchase a Net Leased property by putting twenty to twenty-five percent down and obtaining a long-term loan for the balance, thereby leveraging their available cash and also receiving monthly income (the difference between their Tenant's rent payment and their mortgage note).

But although this income is highly tax-sheltered through the note's interest payment plus the building's depreciation, there will still be some tax due on the monthly profits. Some investors, however, already have an adequate income and desire to retain a Net Leased property in their portfolio but are not seeking additional cash. They may also be anxious to avoid an increased capital gains tax burden. There is a solution to this dilemma: It is called a "Zero."

The investor with strong credit and an excellent relationship with his lender can further leverage his cash outlay while almost totally eliminating any additional capital gains tax obligation by paying only ten percent down and borrowing ninety percent. In this scenario, the interest payments on his note will normally equal the rental payments from his Tenant. Since the two payments are equal and offsetting there will be no monthly cash profit and therefore no capital gains tax.

These properties are called "Zero Cash Flow Properties." Many investors who are not looking for additional income hold this type of loan in their portfolios until their note is completely paid off by the Tenant's monthly rent. The property will then be owned "free and clear" in their estate.

This strategy works especially well in the beginning years of the investor's ownership of his property. But over time, because of the pay-down of the interest portion of the note plus the Tenant's rent increases and/or percentage rent, there will start to be a taxable monthly profit. And although the capital gains tax on this profit may be minimal, the investor may still wish to have none. There is a solution for this too: The 1031 Tax Deferred Exchange.

By year eight or so, with the equity buildup on the note, the rent increases, the possible appreciation on the value of the property and the quality of the Tenant the investor should be able to execute a very favorable Tax Deferred Exchange to another Net Leased property. He will then be able to start the procedure all over again with a new ninety percent loan, a new depreciation schedule, a new Zero Cash Flow property, and an even more valuable Armchair addition to his portfolio.

EPILOGUE

By now you have gained a thorough understanding of Net Lease investing and I hope you agee that it separates "investment" from "work" and is indeed not "too good to be true." As Donald Trump has said, "More millionaires have been made through real estate than any other type of investment." This book was written to help you become one of them.

I would welcome your comments regarding this book or the experiences you may have encountered in your quest for the perfect Armchair Investment. I am looking forward to hearing from you.

HANK LEVINE

GLOSSARY

GLOSSARY

Absolute NNN Lease
A Lease which ads the Tenant's obligation for casualty (fire and wind damage) plus Eminent Domain in addition to all other fixed expenses (taxes, insurance and maintenance). Under no circumstances can the Tenant cancel the Lease. Also referred to as the "hell or high water" Lease.

Adjustable Rate Mortgage (ARM)
A bank loan in which the interest rate, normally much lower than that of a fixed-rate loan, can be increased over time. It usually has an *annual* "cap" and an overall *maximum* "cap" (called a "ceiling") by which the rate can be adjusted to bring it in line with current market rates.

Assumable Loan
The right to take over the loan payments on a previous property owner's debt.

Balloon
The option a lending institution will retain to increase the percentage rate on a long-term permanent loan, usually at the end of its fifth year. Also known as a "Five Year Call."

Break Point
The dollar amount achieved by a Tenant which will obligate him to begin to pay a fixed percentage of his gross

annual sales to the Landlord in addition to his monthly rent.

CAP Rate

Short for "Capitalization Rate"; the percentage return on an investor's initial cash outlay or cash down payment. Calculated by dividing the annual rent payment by the purchase price of the property.

Cash On Cash

The return on an investor's initial cash outlay or cash down payment expressed in dollars.

Commencement Date

In a commercial Lease, the initial date when the Tenant started to pay rent.

Credit Tenant (Investment Grade Tenant)

A large national or regional Retail Chain or Corporation whose credit rating is such that it has the ability to meet long-term Lease obligations regardless of general economic conditions. It will usually have a history of excellent earnings, longevity and a superior current financial standing. Often a "Fortune 500" company.

Double Net (NN)

A Lease in which the Tenant pays taxes and insurance, but obligates the Landlord to pay for some parts of the property's upkeep, most commonly its structural elements (foundation, outside walls, and roof).

Due Diligence

The period of the buyer's investigation (usually 30 days) prior to his confirmation of the purchase of a Net Leased property. Includes approval of the Lease, the location, conditions of the grounds and building and his ability to obtain a favorable loan.

Eminent domain
The right of a government to seize private property for public use in exchange for payment to the owner of fair market value.

Environmental Survey
The inspection of a property by a company licensed and bonded by the state to determine if the soil is free of any hazardous materials.

Equity Buildup
The investor's additional Return On Investment, over a period of years, due to the monthly increase in the "principal" payment of his mortgage.

Exchange Accommodation Titleholder (EAT)
In a Reverse 1031 Exchange, the Qualified Intermediary who holds Title for up to 180 days on a Replacement Property until the Existing Property is sold.

Five Year Call
The option retained by a lending institution to increase the percentage rate on a long-term permanent loan at the end of its fifth year. Also known as a "balloon."

Gross Lease
A Lease in which the Tenant pays a fixed monthly amount to the Landlord and has no financial obligation for property expenses.

Guarantor
The person or entity (corporation) guaranteeing and legally committed to fulfilling all obligations of the Lessee of a commercial property.

Ground Lease
A Lease for a fixed number of years (usually 50 to 99) in which the investor/purchaser owns the land but not the building that is on it ("the improvement"). During its term he receives a monthly or annual payment from the building's occupant. At the Lease's termination all rights to any improvements revert to the landowner.

Holdover Period
The Tenant's ability, with permission of the Lessor, to continue to occupy a property after the termination of its Lease or option period. There will usually be a significant increase in the rent during this period.

Improvement
In real estate, any building or structure located on a given property.

Investment Grade Tenant (see Credit Tenant)

Kick-Out Clause (Termination Clause)

A clause in the Tenant's Lease which gives him the right to terminate the Lease and vacate the property before the end of the primary Lease term in return for a monetary penalty, often about two years rent.

Leasehold Estate
A real estate investment in which the buyer is paid rent monthly by the Tenant for the duration of the Lease, has no Landlord expense or responsibility, but does not own either the land or the building. At its termination his investment is also terminated.

Leverage
The investor's ability to pay a given percentage of cash down on a loan, borrowing the balance and thereby partially purchasing a property with "other people's money."

Letter Of Intent
A proposal from a prospective buyer to a seller offering to purchase his property at a given price. It also includes the buyer's right to a 30-day "Due Diligence Period" to obtain financing and to approve of the property and the existing Lease. It is not legally binding on either party and no Earnest Money is required.

Limited Liability Company (LLC)
An entity combining the characteristics of a corporation and a partnership which carries liability protection for its members and is taxed like a partnership.

Limited Partnership (LP)

An entity comprised of a number of investors ("The Limited Partners") and a "General Partner" who makes the day-to-day operating decisions and submits periodic reports to the Partnership. A Limited Partner incurs no liability beyond the amount of his investment and retains the benefits of appreciation and interest deductions for his pro-rata share of the total value of the properties in the Partnership's portfolio.

Market Rent
In a commercial Lease, the average cost per square foot which a Tenant will pay in rent for a similar type of business in a comparable location.

Mechanic's Lien
An action brought by a tradesman against a commercial business owner for unpaid labor or materials.

Net Lease
General term for those Leases which obligate the Tenant to pay one or all of the major property expenses (taxes, insurance and maintenance).

Net Operating Income (NOI)
The Landlord's annual cash return from a property after deducting all operating expenses. In a Triple Net Lease, since the Tenant is paying all operating expenses, the NOI is the annual rent payment.

NN (Net Net)
Double Net Lease

NNN (Net Net Net)
Triple Net Lease

Outparcel
A property located within the parking lot area of a shopping center which usually contains a major retailer. May be occupied or vacant.

Percentage Rent
The Tenant's obligation to pay a fixed percentage of his annual gross sales to the Landlord in addition to the monthly rent.

Primary Lease Term
The initial term, in years, of a Tenant's Lease.

Qualified Intermediary (QI)
A person or corporation specializing in 1031 Exchanges who holds all proceeds and documents in an escrow-type account throughout the transaction. Also known as a "Facilitator" or "Accommodator."

Quiet Enjoyment
The Tenant's right to occupy the leased property without any undue hindrance or molestation from the Landlord.

REIT (Real Estate Investment Trust)
A corporation, similar to a Mutual Fund, that uses the pooled capital of many investors to purchase and often manage income properties.

Rent Bumps
Periodic rent increases in a commercial Lease.

Return On Investment (ROI)
The return on an investor's cash down-payment expressed either as a percentage or a dollar amount.

Right of Assignment
The Lessee's right, with permission of the Lessor, to transfer his obligations for the balance of the leasehold period to another party. Also called a Sublease.

Right of Refusal
The Tenant's right, upon notification by the Lessor that the property he is occupying has been sold (or leased) to a third party, to purchase (or continue to Lease) that property at the same terms and conditions offered by a prospective buyer (or Tenant). Also called "Right of First Refusal", the Tenant will usually have 15 to 30 days after notification by the seller to either exercise or waive this right.

Self Directed IRA (SD/IRA)
A retirement account (IRA, SEP, 401(k), Keogh, etc.) which holds investments chosen by the investor, not the Custodian. The company/custodian must specialize in and be set up to administrate a real estate IRA.

Shadow Anchored Center
A shopping center with a major "anchor tenant" such as a Super Wal-Mart, Sam's or Kroger's to draw shoppers to

the other retail establishments located nearby within a common parking area.

Sublease
See "Right of Assignment."

Tax-Deferred Exchange (1031 Exchange)
A procedure for deferring the payment of capital gains tax on the sale of income-producing property by re-investing the proceeds in "like kind" property; i.e. any property held for investment purposes.

Termination Right
The option granted to a Tenant to terminate his Lease and vacate the property before the end of the primary Lease term in return for a monetary penalty, often about two years rent. Also known as a "Kick Out Clause."

Tenants-In-Common
An entity in which multiple investors may get together to purchase a Net Leased property as individual owners. Each partner receives a deed at closing for his own undivided fractional interest in the entire property and has the same rights as a single owner. His share of the property's income is in proportion to the amount of his investment.

Trade Fixture
Items utilized by the Lessee in the normal course of his business. At the end of the Lease period they are usually permitted, even if attached, to be removed.

Triple Net Lease (NNN)
A Lease in which the Tenant is responsible for all taxes, insurance and maintenance. The Landlord has no expense or responsibility, giving him what is known as an "Armchair Investment."

Zero Cash Flow Property (Zero)
A Net Leased property in which the investor does not desire a monthly cash return or its resulting capital gains tax. Achieved by obtaining a loan in which the investor pays only 10% down, borrowing 90%. The Tenant's rent payment will usually equal the interest payment on the loan, thereby producing no monthly cash profit.

INDEX

NOTES

NOTES

About The Author

The name Hank Levine on the cover of this book may look familiar to you. If you are a collector of 45 RPM and LP records from the 60s  and 70s you may have seen it on numerous record labels and album jackets. Hank was one of Hollywood's leading composer/arrangers of this period, writing the background music for a number of movies and working with such artists as Ann-Margret, Sammy Davis Jr., Glen Campbell, Wayne Newton and Big Band legends Harry James and Stan Kenton.

Relocating to Nashville in the 70s he recorded with many of country music's legendary performers including Johnny Cash, Chet Atkins, Loretta Lynn and Dolly Parton. He was musical director of the Hee Haw TV Show, Nashville's Opryland Theme Park and has written for and conducted the Nashville Symphony and the London Symphony Orchestra.

Throughout this period Hank was also deeply involved in real estate as an investor, buying and selling commercial properties for his own portfolio. By the early 90s, as the music industry underwent a complete transformation, he decided to make Commercial Real Estate brokerage his full-time profession.

Guided by his own experiences, he examines every transaction in behalf of his clients from the buyer's viewpoint, recommending only those properties that he, as an investor, would purchase. His own Triple Net purchase in 2001 of a 23,000 square foot office/warehouse in Nashville leased by General Electric confirmed his feeling that Net Leased properties are the safest, least labor-intensive and most financially-rewarding real estate investments available.

That prompted his decision to specialize exclusively in Net Leased and 1031 Exchange properties in his Hendersonville, Tennessee brokerage. He decided to write this book when he discovered that there is little information available to new investors looking for the low-risk and steady returns of expense and management-free Triple Net properties leased to major retailers.

To receive information about currently available Net Leased properties or about Hank's Net Lease Workshops for groups and individuals you can log onto his website, **www.ArmchairRealEstate.net** or you may write to Hank at Commercial Investment Associates, P.O. Box 532, Hendersonville, TN 37077.

Purchase Information

To purchase additional copies of this book send a check or money order for $19.95 plus $3.50 for shipping and handling to:

Hollyhill Publishing
P.O. Box 532
Hendersonville, TN 37077

Books shipped by USPS. Please allow 2 to 3 weeks for delivery. 15% discount for orders of 10 or more books.

Sales tax: Please add 9.25% ($1.85) for books shipped to Tennessee addresses.

For information about Hank Levine's Net Lease Workshops you may log onto his website, **www.ArmchairRealEstate.net**. Or you can contact him by mail at Commercial Investment Associates at the above address.